Letters-Fifth Series

by

Swami Vivekananda

Letters-Fifth Series

by Swami Vivekananda

ISBN: 978-93-59393-54-4

Published by

DOUBLE 9 BOOKS

2/13-B, Ansari Road
Daryaganj, New Delhi – 110002
info@double9books.com
www.double9books.com
Tel. 011-40042856

ABOUT THE AUTHOR

Swami Vivekananda was born Narendranath Datta in India on January 12, 1863. He died on July 4, 1902, and was the most important student of the Indian saint Ramakrishna. He was an important part of bringing Vedanta and Yoga to the West. He is also charged with making people more aware of other religions and making Hinduism a major world religion. Vivekananda had a lot of success at the Parliament. In the years that followed, he gave hundreds of lectures across the United States, England, and Europe to spread the main ideas of Hinduism. He also started the Vedanta Society of New York and the Vedanta Society of San Francisco, which is now the Vedanta Society of Northern California. Both of these groups became the basis for Vedanta Societies in the West. Vivekananda was one of the most important philosophers and social reformers in India at the time. He was also one of the most successful and powerful Vedanta missionaries in the West.People now think of him as one of the most important people in modern India and Hinduism. Mahatma Gandhi said that after reading Vivekananda's works, he loved his country a thousand times more.

CONTENTS

I

(Translated from Bengali)

To Balaram Bose

Glory to Ramakrishna

GHAZIPUR

February 6, 1890

RESPECTED SIR,

I have talked with Pavhari Baba. He is a wonderful saint — the embodiment of humility, devotion, and Yoga. Although he is an orthodox Vaishnava, he is not prejudiced against others of different beliefs. He has tremendous love for Mahâprabhu Chaitanya, and he [Pavhari Baba] speaks of Shri Ramakrishna as "an incarnation of God". He loves me very much, and I am going to stay here for some days at his request.

Pavhari Baba can live in Samâdhi for from two to six months at a stretch. He can read Bengali and has kept a photograph of Shri Ramakrishna in his room. I have not yet seen him face to face, since he speaks from behind a door, but I have never heard such a sweet voice. I have many things to say about him but not just at present.

Please try to get a copy of *Chaitanya-Bhâgavata* for him and send it immediately to the following address: Gagan Chandra Roy, Opium Department, Ghazipur. Please don't forget.

Pavhari Baba is an ideal Vaishnava and a great scholar; but he is reluctant to reveal his learning. His elder brother acts as his attendant, but even he is not allowed to enter his room.

Please send him a copy of *Chaitanya-Mangala* also, if it is still in print. And remember that if Pavhari Baba accepts your presents, that will be your great fortune. Ordinarily, he does not accept anything from anybody. Nobody knows what he eats or even what he does.

Please don't let it be known that I am here and don't send news of anyone to me. I am busy with an important work.

Your servant,

NARENDRA

II

(Translated from Bengali)

To Balaram Bose

Glory to Ramakrishna

GHAZIPUR

February 11, 1890

RESPECTED SIR

I have received your book. In Hrishikesh, Kali [Swami Abhedananda] has had a relapse and is again suffering from what seems to be malaria. Once it comes, the fever does not easily leave those who have never had it before. I too suffered the same way when I first had the attack of fever. Kali has never had the fever before. I have not received any letter from Hrishikesh. Where is . . . ?

I am suffering terribly from a backache which began in Allahabad. I had recovered from it some time back, but it has recurred. So I will have to stay here awhile longer because of my back and also because Babaji [Pavhari Baba] has requested it.

What you have written about uncooked bread is true. But a monk dies that way, not like the breaking of a cup and saucer. This time I am not going to be overcome by weakness in any way. And if I die, that will be good for me. It is better to depart from this world very soon.

Your servant,

NARENDRA

III

(Translated from Bengali)

To Balaram Bose

Salutation to Bhagavan Shri Ramakrishna

GHAZIPUR

February 1890

RESPECTED SIR,

I have received an anonymous letter which I have been unable to trace back to the gigantic soul who wrote it. Indeed, one should pay homage to such a man. He who considers a great soul like Pavhari Baba to be no more than water in a hoof print, he who has nothing to learn in this world and who feels it a disgrace to be taught by any other man — truly, such a new incarnation must be visited. I hope that if the government should discover the identity of this person, he will be handled with special care and be placed in the Alipore garden [zoo]. If you happen to know this man, please ask him to bless me, so that even a dog or a jackal may be my Guru — not to speak of a great soul like Pavhari Baba.

I have many things to learn. My master used to say: "As long as I live, so long do I learn". Also please tell this fellow that unfortunately I do not have the time to "cross the seven seas and thirteen rivers" or to go to Sri Lanka in order to sleep after having put oil in the nostrils.

Your servant,

NARENDRA

P.S. Please have the rose-water brought from Ishan Babu's [Ishan Chandra Mukherjee's] residence if there is delay [in their sending it to the Baranagore Math]. The roses are still not in bloom. The rose-water has just been sent to the residence of Ishan Babu.

IV

(Translated from Bengali)

To Balaram Bose

GHAZIPUR
March 12, 1890

BALARAM BABU,

As soon as you get the railway receipt, please send someone to the railway warehouse at Fairlie Place (Calcutta) to pick up the roses and send them on to Shashi. See that there is no delay in bringing or sending them.

Baburam is going to Allahabad soon. I am going elsewhere.

NARENDRA

PS. Know it for certain that everything will be spoiled if delayed.

NARENDRA

V

(Translated from Bengali)

To Tulsiram Ghosh

GHAZIPUR

10 May 1890

DEAR TULSIRAM:

A basket of roses will be sent to you in a few days at Chitpur. Do you please send them up immediately to Shashi [Swami Ramakrishnananda, at the Baranagore Math]. They would not be sent to the care of Balaram Basu, for there would be such nice delays and that would be death to the flowers. I think if sent to Chitpur, to your depot, it would reach you there at the very place; if not, write sharp. Baburam [Swami Premananda] is here, going up in a day or two to Allahabad. I too am going off from this place very soon. I go perhaps to Bareilly and up. What is Balaram Babu [Balaram Bose] doing?

My Pranâms etc. to you all.

Yours affectionately,

NARENDRA

VI

To Swami Saradananda

Salutation to Bhagavan Ramakrishna

CALCUTTA

32 ASHADHA [JULY 15, 1890]

MY DEAR SHARAT

I am sorry to learn that [Vaikunthanath] Sanyal's habits are as yet not Pucca [firm]; and what about Brahmacharya? I don't understand you. If so, the best thing for you both is to come down and live here. The widow of Mohindra Mukherjee is trying head and heart to erect a Math for you, and Surendranath Mitra has left another thousand so that you are very likely soon to get a beautiful place on the river. As for all the hardships up there, I reserve my own opinions.

It was not at all my intention to come down, only the death of Balaram Bose had made me have a peep here and go back. If the mountains be so bad, there is more than enough place for me; only I leave Bengal. If one does not suit, another will. So that is my determination. Everyone here will be so glad at your return here, and from your letter I see it would be downright injurious to you if you didn't come down. So come down at your earliest opportunity. I will leave this place before this letter reaches you; only I won't go to Almora. I have my own plans for the future and they shall be a secret.

As for Sanyal, I do not see how I can benefit him. Of course, you are at liberty to hold your own opinion about the Sanga [holy company] here. That I can find places Sudrishya [having scenic beauty] and Subhiksha [where alms are available] is enough. Sanga is not much, or, I think, not at all necessary for me.

Yours, etc.,

NARENDRA.

VII

To Mrs. G. W. Hale

MINNEAPOLIS

21 November 1893

DEAR MOTHER,

I reached Madison safely, went to a hotel, and sent a message to Mr. Updike. He came to see me. He is a Congregational and so, of course, was not very friendly at first; but in the course of an hour or so became very kind to me, and took me over the whole place and the University. I had a fine audience and $100. Immediately after the lecture I took the night train to Minneapolis.

I tried to get the clergymen's ticket, but they could not give me any, not being the headquarters. The thing to be done is to get a permit from every head office of every line in Chicago. Perhaps it is possible for Mr. Hale to get the permits for me. If it is so, I hope he will take the trouble to send them over to me to Minneapolis if they can reach me by the 25th, or to Des Moines if by the 29th. Else I would do it the next time in Chicago. I have taken the money in a draft on the bank, which cost me 40¢.

May you be blessed for ever, my kind friend; you and your whole family have made such a heavenly impression on me as I would carry all my life.

Yours sincerely,

VIVEKANANDA

VIII

To Mrs. G. W. Hale

MINNEAPOLIS

24 November 1893.

DEAR MOTHER

I am still in Minneapolis. I am to lecture this afternoon, and the day after tomorrow go to Des Moines.

The day I came here they had their first snow, and it snowed all through the day and night, and I had great use for the arctics. (A waterproof overshoe.) I went to see the frozen Minnehaha Falls. They are very beautiful. The temperature today is 21o below zero, but I had been out sleighing and enjoyed it immensely. I am not the least afraid of losing the tips of my ears or nose.

The snow scenery here has pleased me more than any other sight in this country.

I saw people skating on a frozen lake yesterday.

I am doing well. Hoping this will find you all the same, I remain,

Yours obediently,

VIVEKANANDA

IX

To Mrs. G. W. Hale

DETROIT,

14 February 1894.

DEAR MOTHER,

Arrived safely night before last at 1 o'clock a.m. The train was seven hours late, being blocked by snowdrifts on the way. However, I enjoyed the novelty of the sight: several men cutting and clearing the snow and two engines tugging and pulling was a new sight to me.

Here I met Mr. Bagley, the youngest [Paul F. Bagley], waiting for me at the station; and, it being very late in the night, Mrs. Bagley had retired, but the daughters sat up for me.

They are very rich, kind and hospitable. Mrs. Bagley is especially interested in India. The daughters are very good, educated and good-looking. The eldest gave me a luncheon at a club where I met some of the finest ladies and gentlemen of the city. Last evening there was a reception given here in the house. Today I am going to speak for the first time. Mrs. Bagley is a very nice and kind lady. I hope the lectures will please her. With my love and regards for you all, I remain,

Yours sincerely,

VIVEKANANDA.

PS — I have received a letter from Slayton in reply to that in which I wrote to him that I cannot stay. He gives me hope. What is your advice? I enclose the letter [from Narasimhacharya] in another envelope.

Yours,

X

To Mrs. G. W. Hale

DETROIT,

20 February 1894.

DEAR MOTHER

My lectures here are over. I have made some very good friends here, amongst them Mr. Palmer, President of the late World's Fair. I am thoroughly disgusted with this Slayton business and am trying hard to break loose. I have lost at least $5,000 by joining this man. Hope you are all well. Mrs. Bagley and her daughters are very kind to me. I hope to do some private lecturing here and then go to Ada and then back to Chicago. It is snowing here this morning. They are very nice people here, and the different clubs took a good deal of interest in me.

It is rather wearisome, these constant receptions and dinners; and their horrible dinners — a hundred dinners concentrated into one — and when in a man's club, why, smoking on between the courses and then beginning afresh. I thought the Chinese alone make a dinner run through half a day with intervals of smoking!!

However, they are very gentlemanly men and, strange to say, an Episcopal clergyman and a Jewish rabbi take great interest in me and eulogize me. Now the man who got up the lectures here got at least a thousand dollars. So in every place. And this is Slayton's duty to do for me. Instead, he, the liar, had told me often that he has agents everywhere and would advertise and do all that for me. And this is what he is doing. His will be done. I am going home. Seeing the liking the American people have for me, I could have, by this time, got a pretty large sum. But Jimmy Mills and Slayton were sent by the Lord to stand in the way. His ways are inscrutable.

However, this is a secret. President Palmer has gone to Chicago to try to get me loose from this liar of a Slayton. Pray that he may succeed. Several judges here have seen my contract, and they say it is a shameful fraud and can be broken any moment; but I am a monk — no self-defence. Therefore, I had better throw up the whole thing and go to India.

My love to Harriets, Mary, Isabelle, Mother Temple, Mr. Matthews, Father Pope and you all.

Yours obediently,

VIVEKANANDA.

XI

To Mrs. G. W. Hale

DETROIT

February 22, 1894

DEAR MOTHER

I have got the $200 for the engagements, $175 and $117 by private lectures and $100 as a present from a lady.

This sum will be sent to you tomorrow in cheques by Mrs. Bagley. Today, the banks being closed, we could not do it.

I am going tomorrow to lecture at Ada, Ohio. I do not know whether I will go to Chicago from Ada or not. However, kindly let not Slayton know anything about the rest of the money, as I am going to separate myself from him.

Yours obediently,

VIVEKANANDA.

XII

To Mrs. G. W. Hale

DETROIT,

10 March 1894.

DEAR MOTHER,

Reached Detroit safely yesterday evening. The two younger daughters were waiting for me with a carriage. So everything was all right. I hope the lecture will be a success, as one of the girls said the tickets are selling like hot cakes. Here I found a letter from Mr. Palmer awaiting me with a request that I should come over to his house and be his guest.

Could not go last night. He will come in the course of the day to take me over. As I am going over to Mr. Palmer's, I have not opened the awfully-packed bag. The very idea of repacking seems to me to be hopeless. So I could not shave this morning. However, I hope to shave during the course of the day. I am thinking of going over to Boston and New York just now, as the Michigan cities I can come and take over in summer; but the fashionables of New York and Boston will fly off. Lord will show the way.

Mrs. Bagley and all the family are heartily glad at my return and people are again coming in to see me.

The photographer here has sent me some of the pictures he made. They are positively *villainous* — Mrs. Bagley does not like them at all. The real fact is that between the two photos my face has become so fat and heavy — what can the poor photographers do?

Kindly send over four copies of photographs. Not yet made any arrangement with Holden. (A lecture agent at Detroit.) Everything promises to be very nice. "Ssenator Ppalmer" is a very nice gentleman and very kind to me. He has got a French chef — Lord bless his stomach! I am trying to starve and the whole world is against me!! He used to give the best dinners in all Washington! Hopeless! I am resigned!

I will write more from Mr. Palmer's house.

If the Himalayas become the inkpot, the ocean ink, if the heavenly eternal Devadaroo becomes the pen, and if the sky itself becomes paper, still I would not be able to write a drop of the debt of gratitude I owe to you and yours. Kindly convey my love to the four full notes and the four half notes of the Hale gamut.

May the blessings of the Lord be upon you and yours ever and ever.

Ever yours in grateful affection,

VIVEKANANDA.

XIII

To Mrs. G. W. Hale

DETROIT

16 March 1894

DEAR MOTHER,

Since my last, there has been nothing of interest here. Except that Mr. Palmer is a very hearty, jolly, good old man and very rich. He has been uniformly kind to me. Tomorrow I go back to Mrs. Bagley's because I am afraid she is rather uneasy at my long stay here. I am shrewd enough to know that in every country in general, and America in particular, "she" is the real operator at the nose string.

I am going to lecture here on Monday and in two places near the town on Tuesday and Wednesday. I do not remember the lady you refer me to, and she is in Lynn; what is Lynn, where on the globe its position is — I do not know. I want to go to Boston. What good would it do me by stopping at Lynn? Kindly give me a more particular idea. Nor could I read the name of the lady at whose house you say I met the lady. However, I am in no way very anxious. I am taking life very easy in my natural way. I have no particular wish to go anywhere, Boston or no Boston. I am just in a nice come-what-may mood. Something should turn up, bad or good. I have enough now to pay my passage back and a little sight-seeing to boot. As to my plans of *work*, I am fully convinced that at the rate it is progressing I will have to come back four or five times to put it in any shape.

As to informing others and doing good that way, I have failed to persuade myself that I have really anything to convey to the world. So I am very happy just now and quite at my ease. With almost nobody in this vast house and a cigar between my lips, I am dreaming just now and philosophising upon that *work* fever which was upon me. It is all nonsense. I am nothing, the world is nothing, the Lord alone is the only *worker*. We are simply tools in His hands etc., etc., etc. Have you got the Alaska information? If so, kindly send it to me c/o Mrs. Bagley.

Are you coming to the East this summer? With eternal gratitude and love,

Your son,

VIVEKANANDA.

XIV

To Mrs. G. W. Hale

DETROIT

Tuesday, 27 March 1894

DEAR MOTHER,

Herewith I send two cheques of $114 and $75 to be put in the banks for me. I have endorsed them to your care.

I am going to Boston in a day or two. I have got $57 with me. They will go a long way. Something will turn up, as it always does. I do not know where I go from Boston. I have written to Mrs. [Francis W.] Breed but as yet heard nothing from her. His will be done. Not I but Thou — that is always the motto of my life.

With my eternal gratitude, love, and admiration for Mother Church and all the dignitaries,

I remain your son,

VIVEKANANDA.

XV

To Mrs. G. W. Hale

C/O DR. GUERNSEY

528 FIFTH AVENUE

NEW YORK

2 April 1894

DEAR MOTHER,

I am in New York. The gentleman [Dr. Guernsey] whose guest I am is a very nice and learned and well-to-do man. He had an only son whom he lost last July. Has only a daughter now. The old couple have received a great shock, but they are pure and God-loving people and bear it manfully. The lady of the house is very, very kind and good. They are trying to help me as much as they can and they will do a good deal, I have no doubt.

Awaiting further developments. This Thursday [April 5] they will invite a number of the brainy people of the Union League Club and other places of which the Doctor is a member, and see what comes out of it. Parlour lectures are a great feature in this city, and more can be made by each such lecture than even platform talks in other cities.

It is a very clean city. None of that black smoke tarring everyone in five minutes; and the street in which the Doctor lives is a nice, quiet one.

Hope the sisters are doing well and enjoying their music, both in the opera and the parlour. I am sure I would have appreciated the music at the opera about which Miss Mary wrote to me. I am sure the opera musicians do not show the interior anatomy of their throats and lungs.

Kindly give brother Sam my deep love. I am sure he is bewaring of the vidders. Some of the Baby Bagleys are going to Chicago. They will go to see you, and I am sure you would like them very much.

Nothing more to write. With all respect, love and obedience,

Your son,

VIVEKANANDA.

PS — I have not to ask now for addresses. Mrs. Sherman (Mrs. Bagley's married daughter.) has given me a little book with A., B., C., etc., marks and has written under them all the addresses I need; and I hope to write all the future addresses in the same manner. What an example of self-help I am!!

XVI

To Mrs. G. W. Hale

[C/O DR. EGBERT GUERNSEY

528 FIFTH AVENUE]

NEW YORK

10 April 1894

DEAR MOTHER,

I just now received your letter. I have the greatest regard for the Salvationists; in fact, they and the Oxford Mission gentlemen are the only Christian missionaries for whom I have any regard at all. They live with the people, as the people, and for the people of India. Lord bless them. But I would be very, very sorry of any trick being played by them. I never have heard of any *Lord* in India, much less in *Ceylon*. (Now Sri Lanka.) The people of Ceylon and northern India differ more than Americans and Hindus. Nor is there any connection between the Buddhist priest and the Hindu. Our dress, manners, religion, food, language differ entirely from southern India, much less to speak of Ceylon. You know already that I could not speak a word of Narasimha's language!! Although that was only *Madras*. Well, you have Hindu princesses; why not a Lord, which is not a higher title.

There was a certain Mrs. Smith in Chicago. I met her at Mrs. Stockham's. She has introduced me to the Guernseys. Dr. Guernsey is one of the chief physicians of this city and is a very good old gentleman. They are very fond of me and are very nice people. Next Friday I am going to Boston. I have not been lecturing in New York at all. I will come back and do some lecturing here.

For the last few days I was the guest of Miss Helen Gould — daughter of the rich Gould — at her palatial country residence, an hour's ride from the city. She has one of the most beautiful and large green-houses in the world, full of all sorts of curious plants and flowers. They are Presbyterians, and she is a very religious lady. I had a very nice time there.

I met my friend Mr. Flagg (William Joseph Flagg.) several times. He is flying merrily. There is another Mrs. Smith here who is very rich and pious. She has invited me to dine today.

As for lecturing, I have given up raising money. I cannot degenerate myself any more. When a certain purpose was in view, I could work; with that gone I cannot earn for myself. I have sufficient for going back. I have not tried to earn a penny here, and have refused some presents which friends here wanted to make to me. Especially Flagg — I have refused his money. I had in Detroit tried to refund the money back to the donors, and told them that, there being almost no chance of my succeeding in my enterprise, I had no right to keep their money; but they refused and told me to throw that into the waters if I liked. But I cannot take any more conscientiously. I am very well off, Mother. Everywhere the Lord sends me kind persons and homes; so there is no use of my going into beastly worldliness at all.

The New York people, though not so intellectual as the Bostonians, are, I think, more sincere. The Bostonians know well how to take advantage of everybody. And I am afraid even water cannot slip through their closed fingers!!! Lord bless them!!! I have promised to go and I must go; but, Lord, make me live with the sincere, ignorant and the poor, and not cross the shadow of the hypocrites and tall talkers who, as my Master used to say, are like vultures who soar high and high in their talks, but the heart is really on a piece of carrion on the ground.

I would be the guest of Mrs. Breed for a few days and, after seeing a little of Boston, I would come back to New York.

Hope the sisters are all right and enjoying their concerts immensely. There is not much of music in this city. That is a blessing (?) Went to see Barnum's circus the other day. It is no doubt a grand thing. I have not been as yet downtown. This street is very nice and quiet.

I heard a beautiful piece of music the other day at Barnum's — they call it a Spanish Serenada. Whatever it be, I liked it so much. Unfortunately, Miss Guernsey is not given to much thumping, although she has a good assortment of all the noisy stuffs in the world — and so she could not play it, which I regret ever so much.

Yours obediently,

VIVEKANANDA.

PS — Most probably I will go to Annisquam as Mrs. Bagley's guest. She has got a nice house there this summer. Before that, I will go back to Chicago once more if I can.

XVII

To Mrs. G. W. Hale

C/O MISS FLORENCE GUERNSEY

528 FIFTH AVENUE

NEW YORK

4 May 1894

DEAR MOTHER

Herewith I send over $125 in a cheque upon the 5th Avenue Bank to be deposited at your leisure.

I am going to Boston on Sunday, day after tomorrow, and write to you from Boston. With my love to all the family.

I remain yours truly,

VIVEKANANDA

XVIII

To Mrs. John J. Bagley

HOTEL BELLEVUE

EUROPEAN PLAN

BOSTON

May 8, 1894

DEAR MOTHER,

I have arrived in Boston again. Last afternoon [I] spoke at Mrs. Julia Ward Howe's club — of course for nothing, but it gives me a prestige. I saw there Mrs. [Ednah Dean] Cheney. Would you not write a letter to her for me? Although I told her I had a card from you, I think a letter is better.

Yours truly,

VIVEKANANDA

XIX

To Mrs. G. W. Hale

HOTEL BELLEVUE, EUROPEAN PLAN

BEACON STREET, BOSTON

11 May, 1894

DEAR MOTHER,

I have been since the 7th, lecturing here every afternoon or evening. At Mrs. Fairchild's I met the niece of Mrs. Howe. She was here today to invite me to dinner with her today. I have not seen Mr. Volkinen as yet. Of course, the pay for lecture is here the poorest, and everybody has an axe to grind. I got a long letter full of the prattles of the babies. Your city, i.e. New York, pays far better than Boston, so I am trying to go back there. But here one can get work almost every day.

I think I want some rest. I feel as if I am very much tired, and these constant journeyings to and fro have shaken my nerves a little, but hope to recoup soon. Last few days I have been suffering from cold and slight fever and lecturing for all that; hope to get rid of it in a day or two.

I have got a very nice gown at $30. The colour is not exactly that of the old one, but cardinal, with more of yellow — could not get the exact old colour even in New York.

I have not much to write, for it is the repetition of the old story: talking, talking, talking. I long to fly to Chicago and shut up my mouth and give a long rest to mouth and lungs and mind. If I am not called for in New York, I am coming soon to Chicago.

Yours obediently,

VIVEKANANDA.

XX

To Mrs. G. W. Hale

HOTEL BELLEVUE EUROPEAN PLAN

BEACON STREET, BOSTON

14 May, 1894

DEAR MOTHER,

Your letter was so, so pleasing instead of being long; I enjoyed every bit of it.

I have received a letter from Mrs. Potter Palmer (Social queen of Chicago who made Swami Vivekananda's acquaintance at the Parliament of Religions, in which she had been active. Vide Complete Works, VI.) asking me to write to some of my countrywomen about their society etc. I will see her personally when I come to Chicago; in the meanwhile I will write her all I know. Perhaps you have received $125 sent over from New York. Tomorrow I will send another $100 from here. The Bostonians want to grind their own axes!!

Oh, they are so, so dry – even girls talk dry metaphysics. Here is like our *Benares* where all is dry, dry metaphysics!! Nobody here understands "my Beloved". Religion to these people is reason, and horribly stony at that. I do not care for anybody who cannot love my "Beloved". Do not tell it to Miss Howe – she may be offended.

The pamphlet I did not send over because I do not like the quotations from the Indian newspapers – especially, they give a haul over coal to somebody. Our people so much dislike the Brâhmo Samâj that they only want an opportunity to show it to them. I dislike it. Any amount of enmity to certain persons cannot efface the good works of a life. And then they were only children in Religion. They never were much of religious men – i.e. they only wanted to talk and reason, and did not struggle to see the Beloved; and until one does that I do not say that he has any religion. He may have books, forms, doctrines, words, reasons, etc., etc., but not religion;

for that begins when the soul feels the necessity, the want, the yearning after the "Beloved", and never before. And therefore our society has no right to expect from them anything more than from an ordinary "house-holder".

I hope to come to Chicago before the end of this month. Oh, I am so tired.

Yours affectionately,

VIVEKANANDA.

XXI

To Mrs. G. W. Hale

541 DEARBORN AVENUE

CHICAGO

9 June 1894

DEAR MOTHER,

We are all doing very well here. Last night the sisters (The daughters of Mrs. Hale: Mary and Harriet.) invited me and Mrs. Norton and Miss Howe and Mr. Frank Howe. We had a grand dinner and softshell crab and many other things, and a very nice time. Miss Howe left this morning.

The sisters and Mother Temple (Mrs. James Matthews, Mr. Hale's sister.) are taking very good care of me. Just now I am going to see my "oh-my-dear" Gandhi. Narasimha was here yesterday; he wanted to go to Cincinnati where he says he has more chances of success than anywhere else in the world. I gave him the passage, and so I hope I have got the white elephant out of my hands for the time being. How is Father Pope doing now? Hope he has been much benefited by the mudfish business.

I had a very beautiful letter from Miss Guernsey of New York, giving you her regards. I am going downtown to buy a new pair of shoes as well as to get some money, my purse having been made empty by Narasimha.

Nothing more to write. Yes, we went to see the "Charley's Aunt". I nearly killed myself with laughing. Father Pope will enjoy it extremely. I had never seen anything so funny.

Yours affectionately,

VIVEKANANDA.

XXII

To Mrs. G. W. Hale

NEW YORK

28 June 1894

DEAR MOTHER,

Arrived safely two hours ago. Landsberg was waiting at the station. Came to Dr. Guernsey's house. Nobody was there except a servant. I took a bath and strolled with Landsberg to some restaurant where I had a good meal. Then, I have just now returned to Landsberg's rooms in the Theosophical Society and am writing you this letter.

I haven't been to see my other friends yet. After a good and long rest through the night I hope to see most of them tomorrow. My Love to you all. By the by, somebody stepped on my umbrella on board the train and broke its nose off.

Your affectionate son,

VIVEKANANDA.

PS — I have not settled myself. So as to direct letters to me, they can be directed c/o Leon Landsberg, 144 Madison Ave., New York.

XXIII

To Mrs. G. W. Hale

C/O LEON LANDSBERG

144 MADISON AVENUE

NEW YORK

1 July 1894

DEAR MOTHER,

Hope you are settled down in peace by this time. The babies are doing well in Mudville (Kenosha, Wisconsin) — in their nunnery, I am sure. It is very hot here, but now and then a breeze comes up which cools it down. I am now with Miss [Mary A.] Phillips. Will move off from here on Tuesday to another place.

Here I find a quotation from a speech by Sir Monier Williams, professor of Sanskrit in the Oxford University. It is very strange as coming from one who every day expects to see the whole of India converted to Christianity. "And yet it is a remarkable characteristic of Hinduism that it neither requires nor attempts to make converts. Nor is it at present by any means decreasing in numbers, nor is it being driven out of the field by two such proselytizing religions as Mahomedanism [sic] and Christianity. On the contrary, it is at present rapidly increasing. And far more remarkable than this is that, it is all-receptive, all-embracing and all-comprehensive. It claims to be the one religion of humanity, of human nature, of the entire world. It cares not to oppose the progress of Christianity nor of any other religion. For it has no difficulty in including all other religions within its all-embracing arms and ever-widening fold. And in real fact Hinduism has something to offer which is suited to all minds. Its very strength lies in its infinite adaptability to the infinite diversity of human characters and human tendencies. It has its highly spiritual and abstract side suited to the philosophical higher classes. Its practical and concrete side suited to the man of affairs and the man of the world. Its aesthetic and ceremonial side suited to the man of poetic feeling and imagination. Its quiescent and contemplative side suited to the man of peace and lover of seclusion.

"Indeed, the Hindus were Spinozists 2,000 years before the birth of Spinoza, Darwinians centuries before the birth of Darwin, and evolutionists centuries before the doctrine of evolution had been accepted by the Huxleys of our time, and before any word like evolution existed in any language of the world."

This, as coming from one of the staunchest defenders of Christianity, is wonderful indeed. But he seems to have got the idea quite correct.

Now I am going to send up the orange coat today; as for the books that came to me from Philadelphia, I do not think they are worthy of being sent at all. I do not know what I am going to do next. Patiently wait and resign myself unto His guidance — that is my motto. My love to you all.

Your affectionate son,

VIVEKANANDA

XXIV

To Mrs. G. W. Hale

C/O DR. E. GUERNSEY

CEDAR LAWN, FISHKILL ON THE HUDSON

19 July 1894

DEAR MOTHER,

Your kind note reached me here yesterday evening. I am so glad to hear the babies are enjoying. I got the *Interior* and am very glad to see my friend Mazoomdar's (Pratap Chandra Mazumdar.) book spoken of so highly. Mazoomdar is a great and a good man and has done much for his fellow beings.

It is a lovely summer place, this Cedar Lawn of the Guernseys. Miss Guernsey has gone on a visit to Swampscott. I had also an invitation there, but I thought [it] better to stay here in the calm and silent place full of trees and with the beautiful Hudson flowing by and mountain in the background.

I am very thankful for Miss Howe's suggestion, and I am also thinking of it. Most probably I will go to England very soon. But between you and me, I am a sort of mystic and cannot move without *orders*, and that has not come yet. Mr. [Charles M.] Higgins, a rich young lawyer and inventor of Brooklyn, is arranging some lectures for me. I have not settled whether I will stop for them or not.

My eternal thanks to you for your kindness. My whole life cannot repay my debt to you. (Original letter: your debt.) You may see from the letter from Madras that there is not a word about Narasimha. What can I do more? I did not get the cheque cashed yet, for there was no necessity. Miss Phillips was very kind to me. She is an old lady, about 50 or more. You need not feel any worry about my being taken care of. The Lord always takes care of His servants; and so long as I am really His servant and not the world's, I am very confident of getting everything that would be good for me. The Guernseys love me very much, and there are many families in New York and Brooklyn who would take the best care of me.

I had a beautiful letter from Mr. Snell, saying that a sudden change for the better has taken place in his fortunes and offering me thrice the money I lent him as a contribution to my work. And he also has beautiful letters from Dharmapala and others from India. But, of course, I politely refused his repayment.

So far so good. I have seen Mr. [Walter Hines] Page, the editor of the *Forum* here. He was so sorry not to get the article on missionaries. But I have promised to write on other interesting subjects. Hope I will have patience to do so.

I had a letter yesterday from Miss Harriet, (Mrs. Hale's daughter.) from which I learn that they are enjoying Kenosha (A port in southwest Wisconsin, on Lake Michigan.) very much. Lord bless you and yours, Mother Church, for ever and ever. I cannot even express my gratitude to you.

As for me, you need not be troubled in the least. My whole life is that of a *vagabond* — homeless, roving tramp; any fare, good or bad, in any country, is good enough for me.

Yours ever in love and obedience,

SWAMI VIVEKANANDA

XXV

To Mrs. G. W. Hale

SWAMPSCOTT, MASSACHUSETTS

23 July 1894

DEAR MOTHER

I think I have all your questions answered and you are in good humour again.

I am enjoying this place very much; going to Greenacre today or tomorrow and on our way back I intend to go to Annisquam, to Mrs. Bagley's — I have written to her. Mrs. Breed (Mrs. Francis W. Breed of Lynn, Massachusetts.) says, "You are very sensitive".

Now, I fortunately did not cash your check in New York. I wanted to cash it here, when lo! you have not signed your name to it. The Hindu is a dreamer no doubt, but when the Christian dreams he dreams with a vengeance.

Do not be distressed. Somebody gave me plenty of money to move about. I would be taken care of right along. I send herewith the cheque back to you. I had a very beautiful letter from Miss Mary. My love to them.

What is Father Pope doing? Is it very hot in Chicago? I do not care for the heat of this country. It is nothing compared to our India heat. I am doing splendidly. The other day I had the summer cholera; and cramp, etc. came to pay their calls to me. We had several hours nice talk and groans and then they departed.

I am on the whole doing very well. Has the meerschaum pipe reached Chicago? I had nice yachting, nice sea bathing, and am enjoying myself like a duck. Miss Guernsey went home just now. I do not know what more to write.

Lord bless you all.

Affectionately,

VIVEKANANDA

XXVI

To Mrs. G. W. Hale

GREENACRE INN
ELIOT, MAINE
5 August 1894
DEAR MOTHER

I have received your letter and am very much ashamed at my bad memory. I unfortunately forgot all about the cheque. Perhaps you have come to know by this time of my being in Greenacre. I had a very nice time here and am enjoying it immensely. In the fall I am going to lecture in Brooklyn, New York. Yesterday I got news that they have completed all the advertising there. I have an invitation today from a friend in New York to go with him to some mountains north of this state of Maine. I do not know whether I will go or not. I am doing pretty well. Between lecturing, teaching, picnicking and other excitements the time is flying rapidly. I hope you are doing very well and that Father Pope is in good trim. It is a very beautiful spot — this Greenacre — and [I] have very nice company from Boston: Dr. Everett Hale, you know, of Boston, and Mrs. Ole Bull, of Cambridge. I do not know whether I will accept the invitation of my friend of New York or not.

So far only this is sure, that I will go to lecture in New York this coming fall. And Boston, of course, is a good field. The people here are mostly from Boston and they all like me very much. Are you having a good time, and Father Pope? Has your house-painting been finished? The Babies, I am sure, are enjoying their Mudville.

I am in no difficulty for money. I have plenty to eat and drink.

With my best love and gratitude to you and Father Pope and the Babies.

Yours affectionately,

VIVEKANANDA

Excuse this hasty scrawl. The pen is very bad.

The Harrison people sent me two "nasty standing" photos — that is all I have out of them, when they ought to give me 40 minus the 10 or 15 I have got already!!!

XXVII

To Mrs. G. W. Hale

GREENACRE INN

ELIOT, MAINE

8 August 1894

DEAR MOTHER

I have received the letter you sent over to me coming from India.

I am going to leave this place on Monday next for Plymouth [Massachusetts], where the Free Religious Association is holding its session. They will defray my expenses, of course.

I am all right, enjoying nice health, and the people here are very kind and nice to me. Up to date I had no occasion to cash any cheque as everything is going on smoothly. I have not heard anything from the Babies. Hope they are doing well. You also had nothing to write; however, I feel that you are doing well.

I would have gone over to another place, but Mr. Higginson's invitation ought to be attended to. And Plymouth is the place where the fathers of your country first landed. I want, therefore, to see it.

I am all right. It is useless reiterating my love and gratitude to you and yours — you know it all. May the Lord shower His choicest blessings on you and yours.

This meeting is composed of the best professors of your country and other people, so I must attend it; and then they would pay me. I have not yet determined all my plans, only I am going to lecture in New York this coming fall; every arrangement is complete for that. They have printed advertisements at their own expense for that and made everything ready.

Give my best love to the Babies, to Father Pope, and believe me ever in gratitude and love,

Your Son,

VIVEKANANDA.

P.S. I am very much obliged to the sisters for asking me to tell them if I want anything. I have no want anyway — I have everything I require and more to spare.

"He never gives up His servants."

My thanks and gratitude eternal to the sisters for their kindness in asking about my wants.

XXVIII

To Mrs. G. W. Hale

C/O MRS. J. J. BAGLEY, ANNISQUAM

20 August 1894

DEAR MOTHER

Your letters just now reached me. I had some beautiful letters from India. The letter from Ajit Singh (The Raja of Khetri, a very devoted disciple of the Swami.) shows that the phonograph has not reached yet, and it was dated 8th June. So I do not think it is time yet to get an answer. I am not astonished at my friends' asking Cook & Sons to hunt for me; I have not written for a long time.

I have a letter from Madras which says they will soon send money to Narasimha (Narasimhacharya. Vide the letter dated February 14, 1894.) – in fact, as soon as they get a reply to their letter written to Narasimha. So kindly let Narasimha know it. The photographs have not reached me – except two of Fishkill when I was there last. Landsberg (Leon Landsberg. Vide the letter dated June 28, 1894.) has kindly sent over the letters. From here I will probably go over to Fishkill. The meerschaum was not sent over by me direct, but I left it to the Guernseys. And they are a lazy family in that respect.

I have beautiful letters from the sisters.

By the by, your missionaries try to make me a malcontent before the English government in India, and the Lieutenant Governor of Bengal in a recent speech hinted that the recent revival of Hinduism was against the government. Lord bless the missionary. Everything is fair in love and (religion?).

The word *Shri* means "of good fortune", "blessed", etc. Paramahamsa is a title for a Sannyâsi who has reached the goal, i.e. realized God. Neither am I blessed nor have I reached the goal; but they are courteous, that is all. I will soon write to my brothers in India. I am so lazy, and I cannot send over the newspaper nonsense day after day.

I want a little quiet, but it is not the will of the Lord, it seems. At Greenacre I had to talk on an average 7 to 8 hours a day — that was rest, if it ever was. But it was of the Lord, and that brings vigour along with it.

I have not much to write, and I do not remember anything of what I said or did all these places over. So I hope to be excused.

I will be here a few days more at least, and therefore I think it would be better to send over my mail here.

I have now almost become dizzy through the perusal of a heavy and big mail, so excuse my hasty scrawl.

Ever affectionately yours,

SWAMI VIVEKANANDA.

XXIX

To Mrs. G. W. Hale

ANNISQUAM

23 August 1894

DEAR MOTHER

The photographs reached safely yesterday. I cannot tell exactly whether Harrison ought to give me more or not. They had sent only two to me at Fishkill — not the pose I ordered, though.

Narasimha has perhaps got his passage by this time. He will get it soon, whether his family gives him the money or not. I have written to my friends in Madras to look to it, and they write me they will.

I would be very glad if he becomes a Christian or Mohammedan or any religion that suits him; but I am afraid for some time to come none will suit our friend. Only if he becomes a Christian he will have a chance to marry again, even in India — the Christians there permitting it. I am so sorry to learn that it is the "bondage of heathen India" that, after all, was the cause of all this mischief. We learn as we live. So we were all this time ignorantly and blindly blaming our much suffering, persecuted, saintly friend Narasimha, while all the fault was really owing to the "bondage of heathen India"!!!!

But to give the devil his due, this heathen India has been supplying him with money to go on a spree again and again. And this time too "heathen India" will [take] or already has taken our "enlightened" and persecuted friend from out of his present scrape, and not "Christian America"!! Mrs. Smith's plan is not bad after all — to turn Narasimha into a missionary of Christ. But unfortunately for the world, many and many a time the flag of Christ has been entrusted to such hands. But I would beg to add that he will then be only a missionary of Smithian American Christianity, not Christ's. Arrant humbug! That thing to preach Lord Jesus!!! Is He in want of men to uphold His banner? Pooh! the very idea is revolting. Do good to India indeed! Thank your charity and call back your dog — as the tramp said. Keep such good workers for America. The Hindus will have a quarantine against all such [outcasting] to protect their society. I heartily advise Narasimha to become a *Christian* — I beg your pardon, a convert to *Americanism* — because I am sure such a jewel is unsaleable in poor India. He is welcome to anything that will fetch a price. I know the gentleman whom you name perfectly well, and you may give him any information about me you like. I do not care for sending scraps and getting a boom for me. And these friends from India bother me enough for newspaper nonsense. They are very devoted, faithful and holy friends. I have not much of these scraps now. After a long search I found a bit in a *Boston Transcript*. I send it over to you. This public life is such a botheration. I am nearly daft.

Where to fly? In India I have become horribly public — crowds will follow me and take my life out. I got an Indian letter from Landsberg. Every ounce of fame can only be bought at the cost of a pound of peace and holiness. I never thought of that before. I have become entirely disgusted with this blazoning. I am disgusted with myself. Lord will show me the way to peace and purity. Why, Mother, I confess to you: no man can live in an atmosphere of public life, even in religion, without the devil of competition now and then thrusting his head into the serenity of his heart. Those who are trained to preach a *doctrine* never feel it, for they never knew *religion*. But those that are after *God*, and not after the world, feel at once that every bit of name and fame is at the cost of their purity. It is so much gone from that ideal of perfect *unselfishness*, perfect disregard of gain or name or fame. Lord help me. Pray for me, Mother. I am very much disgusted with myself. Oh, why the world be so that one cannot do anything without putting himself to the front; why cannot one act hidden and unseen and unnoticed? The world has not gone one step beyond idolatry yet. They cannot act from ideas, they cannot be led by ideas. But they want the person, the man. And any man that wants to do something must pay the penalty — no hope. This nonsense of the world. Shiva, Shiva, Shiva.

By the by, I have got such a beautiful edition of Thomas à Kempis. How I love that old monk. He caught a wonderful glimpse of the "behind the veil" — few ever got such. My, that is religion. No humbug of the world. No shilly-shallying, tall talk, conjecture — I presume, I believe, I think. How I would like to go out of this piece of painted humbug they call the beautiful world with Thomas à Kempis — beyond, beyond, which can only be felt, never expressed.

That is religion. Mother, there is God. There all the saints, prophets and incarnations meet. Beyond the Babel of Bibles and Vedas, creeds and crafts, dupes and doctrines — where is all light, all love, where the miasma of this earth can never reach. Ah! who will take me thither? Do you sympathize with me, Mother? My soul is groaning now under the hundred sorts of bondage I am placing on it. Whose India? Who cares? Everything is His. What are we? Is He dead? Is He sleeping? He, without whose command a leaf does not fall, a heart does not beat, who is nearer to me than my own self. It is bosh and nonsense — to do good or do bad or do fuzz. We do nothing. We are not. The world is not. He is, He is. Only He is. None else is. He is.

Om, the one without a second. He in me, I in Him. I am like a bit of glass in an ocean of light. I am not, I am not. He is, He is, He is.

Om, the one without a second.

Yours ever affectionately,

VIVEKANANDA.

XXX

To Mrs. G. W. Hale

ANNISQUAM

DATE DO NOT KNOW

[Postmarked: August 28, 1894]

DEAR MOTHER

I have been for three days at Magnolia. Magnolia is one of the most fashionable and beautiful seaside resorts of this part. I think the scenery is better than that of Annisquam. The rocks there are very beautiful, and the forests run down to the very edge of the water. There is a very beautiful pine forest. A lady of Chicago and her daughter, Mrs. Smith and Mrs. Sawyer, were the friends that invited me up there. They had also arranged a lecture for me, out of which I got $43. I met a good many Boston people — Mrs. Smith Junior, who said she knows Harriet, and Mrs. Smith the elder, [who] knows you well.

In Boston the other day I met a Unitarian clergyman who said he lives next to you in Chicago. I have unfortunately forgotten his name. Mrs. Smith is a very nice lady and treated me with all courtesy. Mrs. Bagley is kind as ever, and I will have to remain here a few days more, I am afraid. Prof. Wright and I are having a good time. Prof. Bradley of Evanston has gone home. If you ever meet him at Evanston, give him my best love and regards. He is really a spiritual man.

I do not find anything more to write.

Some unknown friend has sent me from New York a fountain pen. So I am writing with it to test it. It is working very smoothly and nicely as you can judge from the writing. Perhaps Narasimha's difficulties have been settled by this time, and "heathen India" has helped him out yet, I hope.

What is Father Pope doing? What the Babies are doing and where are they? What news of our Sam? Hope he is prospering. Kindly give him my best love. Where is Mother Temple now?

Well, after all, I could fill up two pages. Yes, there was a Miss Barn (?) who said she met me at your house. She is a young lady of Chicago.

Magnolia is a good bathing place and I had two baths in the sea. A large concourse of men and women go to bathe there every day — the most part men. And strange, women do not give up their coat of mail even while bathing. That is how these mailclad she-warriors of America have got the superiority over men.

Our Sanskrit poets lavish all the power of expression they have upon the soft body of women — the Sanskrit word for women is "Komala", the soft body; but the mailclad ones of this country are "armadillas", I think. You cannot imagine how ludicrous it appears to a foreigner who never saw it before. Shiva, Shiva.

Now Narasimha's Mrs. Smith does not torture you anymore with letters, I hope. Did I tell you I met your friend Mrs. H. O. Quarry at Swampscott? — she can swamp a house for all that, not to speak of a cott — and that I met there the woman that pulls by the nose Mr. Pullman? And I also heard there the best American singer, (Miss Emma Thursby.) they said — she sang beautifully; she sang "Bye Baby Bye". I am having a very, very good time all the time, Lord be praised.

I have written to India not to bother me with constant letters. Why, when I am travelling in India nobody writes to me. Why should they spend all their superfluous energy in scrawling letters to me in America? My whole life is to be that of a wanderer — here or there or anywhere. I am in no hurry. I had a foolish plan in my head unworthy of a Sannyasin. I have given it up now and mean to take life easy. No indecent hurry. Don't you see, Mother Church? You must always remember, Mother Church, that I cannot settle down even at the North Pole, that wander about I must — that is my vow, my religion. So India or North Pole or South Pole — don't care where. Last two years I have been travelling among races whose language even I cannot speak. "I have neither father nor mother nor brothers nor sisters nor friends nor foes, nor home nor country — a traveller in the way of *eternity*, asking no other help, seeking no other help but God."

Yours ever affectionately,

VIVEKANANDA.

XXXI

To Mrs. G. W. Hale

[GLOUCESTER, MASSACHUSETTS]

4 September 1894

DEAR MOTHER

The bundle was the report of the meeting. Hope you will succeed in publishing some in the Chicago papers.

Here is a letter from Dewanji to you which will explain his sending a pamphlet to Mr. Hale. The rugs are coming. When they come, take them in, even paying the duty if any. I will pay it to you afterwards. I have plenty of money, more than $150 in pocket. Will get more tonight. Here are some newspaper clippings, and an *Indian Mirror* I will send later on. Some have been sent to Mr. Barrows; don't hope he will give them publicity. Now for your Mrs. Bartlett.

I am in haste. [Will] write more with the clippings. Write to me always, kind Mother — I become very anxious when I do not hear from you. Write, whether I reply sharp or not.

Your son,

VIVEKANANDA

XXXII

To Mrs. G. W. Hale

ANNISQUAM

5 September 1894

DEAR MOTHER

The news of the arrival of the phonograph from Khetri has not come yet. But I am not anxious, because I just now got another letter from India wherein there is no mention of the photographs I sent, showing that parcels reach later than letters.

Herewith I send you an autograph letter of H.H. the Maharaja of Mysore, the chief Hindu king in India. You may see on the map [that] his territory occupies a very large portion of southern India.

I am very glad that he is slowly being gained over to my side. If he wills, he can set all my plans to work in five days. He has an income of $150 million dollars; think of that.

May Jagadamba [the Mother of the Universe] turn his mind towards the good work. He says he quite appreciates my good words — they were about my plans for educating the poor. Hope he will soon show it in material shape.

My love to all. Why the babies do not prattle?

Your son,

VIVEKANANDA

XXXIII

To Mrs. G. W. Hale

HOTEL BELLEVUE, EUROPEAN PLAN

BEACON STREET, BOSTON

12 September 1894

DEAR MOTHER

I hope you will immediately send me over the little scrap from the *Indian Mirror* about my Detroit lectures which I sent you.

Yours,

VIVEKANANDA

XXXIV

To Mrs. G. W. Hale

HOTEL BELLEVUE

BEACON STREET, BOSTON

13 September 1894

DEAR MOTHER

Your very kind note came just now. I was suffering for the last few days from cold and fever. I am all right now. I am glad all the papers reached you safe. The newspaper clippings are with Mrs. Bagley; only a copy has been sent over to you. By the by, Mrs. Bagley becomes jealous if I send away everything to you. That is between you and me. The *Indian Mirror* is with Prof. Wright, and he will send it over to you. There is yet no news of the phonograph. Wait one week more and then we will enquire. If you see a letter with the Khetri stamp, then surely the news is coming. I do not smoke one third as much as I used to when Father Pope's eternal box was ready and open day and night. Haridasbhai is to be addressed as Shri only. On the envelope, Dewan Bahadoor ought to be written, as that is a title. Perhaps the note from the Maharaja of Mysore has reached you by this time.

I will remain a few days yet in Boston and the vicinity. The bank book is in the bank. We did not take it out, but the cheque book is with me. I am going to write out my thoughts on religion; in that, no missionaries have any place. I am going to lecture in New York in autumn, but I like teaching small circles better, and there will be enough of that in Boston.

The rugs I wanted to be sent from India; and they will come from Punjab, where the best rugs are made.

I had a beautiful letter from Sister Mary. (Mary Hale.)

Narasimha must have got money or passage by this time, and his people have taken care to send him Thomas Cook's passage from place to place. I think he is gone now.

I do not think the Lord will allow his servant to be inflated with vanity at the appreciation of his countrymen. I am glad that they appreciate me — not for my sake, but that I am firmly persuaded that a man is never improved by abuse but by praise, and so with nations. Think how much of abuse has been quite unnecessarily hurled at the head of my devoted, poor country, and for what? They never injured the Christians or their religion or their preachers. They have always been friendly to all. So you see, Mother, every *good word* a foreign nation says to them has such an amount of power for good in India. The American appreciation of my humble work here has really done a good deal of benefit to them. Send a good word, a good thought — at least to the down-trodden, vilified, poor millions of India instead of abusing them day and night. That is what I beg of every nation. Help them if you can; if you cannot, at least cease from abusing them.

I did not see any impropriety in the bathing places at the seashore, but only *vanity* in some: in those that went into water with their corsets on, that was all.

I have not got any copy of the *Inter-Ocean* yet. (A leading Chicago newspaper.)

With my love to Father Pope, babies, and to you, I remain

Your obedient son,

VIVEKANANDA

XXXV

To Mrs. G. W. Hale

HOTEL BELLEVUE

BEACON STREET , BOSTON

19 September 1894

DEAR MOTHER

The huge packet received. It was a few pamphlets sent over to me from my monastery in Calcutta. No news at all about the phonograph. I think it is high time we make them inquire into it.

The two volumes of Todd's [Tod's] history of Rajasthan have been presented to me by Mrs. Potter Palmer. I have asked her to send it over to your care. The babies will like reading it very much, and after they finish I will send it over with my Sanskrit books to Calcutta.

I did not ask you to send me the typewritten news clippings at all, but a little slip I sent over some time ago from the *Indian Mirror*. Perhaps it did not reach you at all. You need not send the typewritten thing at all.

I do not require any clothes here; there are plenty of them. I am taking good care of my cuffs and collars, etc.

I have more clothes than are necessary. Very soon I will have to disburse myself of half of them at least.

I will write to you before I go to India. I am not flying off without giving you due intimation.

Yours,

VIVEKANANDA

P.S. — My love to Babies and Father Pope.

XXXVI

To Mrs. G. W. Hale

HOTEL BELLEVUE

BEACON STREET, BOSTON

24 September 1894

DEAR MOTHER,

I have not heard from you a long while. I am still in Boston and will be a few days more.

I am afraid the phonograph has not reached India at all, or something is the matter with it. Kindly ask Mr. — — to inquire. The receipt is with you on which they will enquire.

Ever affectionately yours,

VIVEKANANDA

XXXVII

To Mrs. G. W. Hale

HOTEL BELLEVUE

BEACON STREET, BOSTON

27 September 1894

DEAR MOTHER

The bundles all came safely. One was newspapers from India. The other was the short sketch of my Master published by Mr. Mazumdar long ago. In the latter bundle there are two sextos or pamphlets. One, my Master's sketch; the other, a short extract to show how what Mr. [Keshab] Chandra Sen and [Pratap Chandra] Mazumdar preached as their "New Dispensation" was stolen from my Master's life. The latter therefore you need not distribute, but I hope you will distribute my Master's life to many good people.

I beg you to send some to Mrs. Guernsey, Fishkill on the Hudson, N.Y.; Mrs. Arthur Smith and Mrs. [Miss Mary A.] Phillips, 19 West 38th Street, New York (both); to Mrs. Bagley, Annisquam, Mass.; and Prof. J. Wright, Professor of Greek, Harvard, Mass.

The newspapers — you may do whatever you like, and I hope you will send any newspaper scrap you get about me to India.

Yours etc.,

VIVEKANANDA

XXXVIII

To Mrs. G. W. Hale

C/O MRS. OLE BULL

168 BRATTLE STREET

CAMBRIDGE, MASS.

5 October 1894

DEAR MOTHER,

I have not heard from you for long. Have you received the huge packages I sent over to you? Have you heard anything about the phonograph from the express office?

I will be with Mrs. Ole Bull a few days, and then I go to New York to Mrs. Guernsey's.

Yours ever affectionately,

VIVEKANANDA

XXXIX

To Mrs. G. W. Hale

C/O MRS. OLE BULL

RIVERVIEW, 168 BRATTLE STREET

CAMBRIDGE, MASS.

[Postmarked: Oct. 10, 1894, 4:30 a.m.]

DEAR MOTHER,

Received two letters from you and a large number from India but none from Khetri.

I am sorry the sisters have got bad colds and more sorry for your getting worried over it. Nothing can make a Christian worry. I hope Narasimha will be a good boy this time forth. Sister Mary is coming to Boston — good. I am going off from here tomorrow to Baltimore. I had enough to pay all my expenses here; and since I am living with Mrs. Bull, there is no expense. She is a rich and highly cultured lady. She has given me $500 for my work or anything I like. As I am not going west very soon, I will have a bank account here in Boston. From Philadelphia I go to Washington, and then I will run between New York and Boston. So I do not think I will be able to see you, except perhaps Sister Mary. I want so very much that Mary will see Mrs. Bull and others of my friends here. I have the fat of the land as usual, and my dinner is cooking very well both here and in India. Do not make it public, Mother — that is between you and me and the babies — and do not worry yourself about anything. All things come to him that waits. I am going to send the greater part of the money I have got to India and then money will come faster. I have always found that the faster I spend, the faster it comes. Nature abhors a vacuum. I am in very good spirits, only you must not stop keeping me informed about yourself, Babies and Father Pope from time to time.

Perhaps you remember the two letters that came from Mysore — I want one of those envelopes with the Mysore King's seal on the outside to be sent to Miss Phillips, 19 West 38th Street, New York.

I cannot go to New York now nor to Chicago, although I had a number of invitations and offers from both the places. I must see now the capital and the other cities. I am in His Hands. If Miss Mary be in Boston, sometime I may hope to see her.

I am glad that Narasimha was never fast — hope he will never be.

From India they always write me to come, come, come. They do not know the secret. I am acting more from here than I will ever do from there.

Kindly send my letters to this address and they will reach me safe wherever I be. This will be one of my homes when I am in Boston.

Lord bless you all, dear Mother.

Yours ever affectionately,

VIVEKANANDA

XL

To Mrs. Ole Bull

1123 SAINT PAUL STREET, BALTIMORE,

17 October 1894.

DEAR MRS. BULL,

I could not find time earlier to write you — I was so incessantly knocking about. We had a nice meeting last Sunday at Baltimore and [are] going to have one more next Sunday. Of course, they do not financially help me a bit; but as I promised to help them and like the idea, I speak for them.

In the letters you sent over from India was an address sent over to me from Calcutta by my fellow citizens for my work here and a number of newspaper cuttings. I will send them on to you later.

Yesterday I went to see Washington and met Mrs. Colville and Miss Young, who were very kind to me.

I am going to speak at Washington again and then will go over to Philadelphia and from there to New York.

Your affectionate Son,

VIVEKANANDA.

XLI

To Miss Emma Thursby

[WASHINGTON, D.C.

26 October 1894]

DEAR MISS THURSBY,

I received your kind note and the introductory letters. I will make it a point to see the ladies and hope to be benefitted much by it.

I had a beautiful letter from Mr. Flagg. I am soon coming to N.Y. where I hope to see you.

With my deepest love and gratitude,

I remain yours faithfully,

VIVEKANANDA

XLII

To Mrs. G. W. Hale

[WASHINGTON, D.C.

October 27, 1894]

DEAR MOTHER,

I received your very kind note and all the India letters just now. I will make it a point to see Mrs. Whitland [?]. I have been very kindly treated by Mrs. [Enoch] Totten.

Will you kindly order 100 photographs from Harrison, and send them over to India to Ramdayal Chakravarty, c/o Swami Ramakrishnananda, Varahanagar Math, Alambazar, Calcutta? I will pay for it when I come to Chicago.

I have nothing especial to write — except I had good treatment everywhere. How I long to give up this life of weariness and blazoning day and night.

I will go from here to New York and will come back to see you in Chicago before I start for England.

Yours etc.,

VIVEKANANDA

XLIII

To Mrs. G. W. Hale

BALTIMORE, [MARYLAND]

3 November 1894

DEAR MOTHER,

I do not know what to say about this phonograph business. It takes six months to go to India!! and the company cannot get an inquiry in another six months!!! American express, indeed!! Well — however, they are bound to make good my money. Mother, do not lose the receipt of the express company.

I am going to New York as soon as possible.

Yours affectionately,

VIVEKANANDA

XLIV

To Mrs. G. W. Hale

NEW YORK

18 November 1894

DEAR MOTHER

I have been very late this time in writing you as Sister Mary has already written to you, no doubt, about me.

The clothes have all reached safe, only I will send over some of the summer and other clothes as it will be impossible to carry the burden all along with me.

The certainty about going to Europe this December has gone; so I am uncertain when I go.

Sister Mary has improved a great deal from what I saw her last. She lives with a number of fox-hunting squires and is quite happy. I hope she will marry one of those fellows with long pockets. I am going again to see her tomorrow at Mrs. Spalding's — I was there last afternoon. I will be in N.Y. this month; then I go to Boston and perhaps will be there all through December. When I was sick in Boston last spring, I went over to Chicago, and not to Detroit as Mrs. Bagley expected. So this time I am going to Detroit first and then to Chicago, if possible. Else I altogether give up the plan of going to the West soon.

There is more chance of working my plans out in the East than in the West, as it now appears.

I have got news of the phonograph — it has reached safe, and the Râjâ wrote to me a very nice letter on that. I have a lot of addresses and other nonsense from India. I have written home to them not to send any more newspapers. My love to the babies at home and I am going to visit the baby abroad.

Mrs. Guernsey has been at death's door. She is now recovering slowly. I have not seen her yet. She is not strong enough to see anybody. Hope she will soon be strong.

My love to Father Pope and everyone.

Your ever affectionate son,

VIVEKANANDA

XLV

To Mrs. G. W. Hale

C/O MRS. OLE BULL
168 BRATTLE STREET
CAMBRIDGE, MASS.
6 December 1894
DEAR MOTHER

I have not heard long from you. What is the matter with you? I am here in Cambridge and will be here for three weeks to come and will have to lecture and hold classes. Here is a Chicago lady, Mrs. [Milward] Adams, who lectures on tone building etc.

Today we had a lecture from Lady Henry Somerset on Woman Suffrage. Miss Willard of Chicago was here and Julia Ward Howe.

Col. Higginson, Dr. [J. Estlin] Carpenter of Eng. and many other friends were present. Altogether it was a grand affair. I have received a letter from India informing me that the phonograph was duly received.

I have sent part of my money to India and intend sending nearly the whole of it very soon. Only, I will keep enough for the passage back. Saw Mother Temple several times in New York. She was kind as usual. So was Mrs. Spalding.

Sister Mary wrote me a letter from Brookline [Massachusetts]. I am sure she would have enjoyed Lady Somerset's lecture so much. I wrote her about it, but I have not heard from her yet.

I will go to see her the first day I get some time. I am very busy. Hope the sisters at home are enjoying themselves. I will try to run into Chicago for a few days if I can.

Please write me all about the holy family as soon as you get time.

Mrs. Guernsey was very ill and still so weak that she cannot get out of her room.

Miss Helen Bagley was seized with diphtheria in New York and suffered a good deal. She has recovered, however, and the Bagleys have gone home to Detroit.

With my Love to you all, I remain,

Ever yours affectionately,

VIVEKANANDA

P.S. — Kindly send my India mail c/o Mrs. Sara Ole Bull, 168 Brattle Street, Cambridge, Mass.

XLVI

To Mrs. G. W. Hale

[CAMBRIDGE , MASS.

21 December 1894]

DEAR MOTHER,

I am glad that Haridas Viharidas (The Dewan of Junagadh.) has sent the rugs. I am afraid they will take a long time to reach here. The Raja (Maharaja Ajit Singh, the Raja of Khetri.) was very much pleased with the phonograph, as he writes, and has heard my voice several times. Hope he will bring it into life.

I have not seen Sister Mary yet, but hope to see her this week as I am going away to New York next Tuesday. Cannot come by any means to Chicago now, for I expect to go to Washington from New York and hope to be pretty busy in New York.

If I can snatch up a few days between the lecture in Brooklyn on the 30th and the next series in New York, I will fly to Chicago for a few days. If I had time just now, it would have been better for me, for the half — fare ticket will expire after this month.

I have been kept very busy here this month so could not go to Boston even for a day. Now I have time and hope to see Sister Mary.

How are the babies at home? Mrs. M. Adams of Chicago, who lectures on voice building and walking etc., has been lecturing here all this time. She is a very great lady in every respect and so intelligent. She knows all of you and likes the "Hale girls" very much. Sister Isabel[le] knows her especially, I think.

Do not you see, Mother — I am determined to work my project out. I *must see the light*. India can cheer alone — but no money. In the East and South I am getting slowly friends who will help me in my work, I am sure, as they have done already. They all like me more and more.

I have made friends of Lady Somerset and Miss Willard, you will be glad to know. So you see, Mother, you are the only attraction in Chicago;

and so long I am in this country, wherever you live is my home. As soon as I have time I will run in to see you and the sisters. But I have no other hopes in the West; nor will you advise me to destroy the *only* hope I have of success in these parts of the country by giving it up and going to Chicago to be idle as the day is long.

Mrs. Bull and a few other ladies here who are helping me on are not only sincere and love me but they have the power to do as leaders of society. Would that you had millions.

With my love to you all,

Your ever affectionate Son,

VIVEKANANDA

XLVII

To Miss Emma Thursby

CHICAGO

541 DEARBORN AVENUE

17 January 1895

DEAR MISS THURSBY,

I am very sorry to learn about the passing on of Mr. Thorp. Mrs. Bull must have felt it deeply. Still he has passed on after a good and useful life. All is for the best.

I have been lecturing every day to a class in Mrs. Adams's rooms at the Auditorium. Today I also lecture there and in the Evening to a class of Miss Josephine Locke's at the Plaza Hotel.

Have you seen Mrs. Peake in New York? She is lecturing to a class at Mrs. Guernsey's.

Miss Locke is as kind as usual. She is enamoured of Mrs. Peake as are many of Miss Locke's friends, you will be glad to learn.

Mrs. Peake has made a very favourable impression on Chicago. So she does wherever she goes.

Mrs. Adams invited me to an organ concert in the Auditorium. She is so good and kind to me. Lord bless her.

I have not seen Mr. Young, nor, I am afraid, [will] I have time to see [him,] as I start for New York on Friday next.

I will hear him once in New York.

I was so busy here these two weeks.

I have got a new scarlet coat but can get no orange here.

Ever with blessings,

Your brother,

VIVEKANANDA

XLVIII

To Professor John H. Wright

54 W. 33 STREET

NEW YORK

1 February 1895

DEAR ADHYAPAKJI,

You must be immersed in your work now; however, taking advantage of your kindness to me, I want to bother you a little.

What was the original Greek idea of the soul, both philosophical and popular? What books can I consult (Translations, of course) to get it?

So with the Egyptians and Babylonians and Jews?

Will you kindly name me the books? I am sure you are perfectly well and so are Mrs. Wright and the children.

Ever gratefully and fraternally,

Yours,

VIVEKANANDA

XLIX

To Mrs. G. W. Hale

54 W. 33., NEW YORK

18 March [February] 1895

DEAR MOTHER,

I am sure you are all right by this time. The babies write from time to time and so I get your news regularly. Miss Mary is in a lecturing mood now — good for her. Hope she will not let her energies fritter away now — a penny saved is a penny gained. Sister Isabel[le] has sent me the French Books and the Calcutta pamphlets have arrived, but the big Sanskrit books ought to come. I want them badly. Make them payable here, if possible, or I will send you the postage.

I am doing very well. Only some of these big dinners kept me late, and I returned home at 2 o'clock in the morning several days. Tonight I am going to one of these. This will be the last of its kind. So much keeping up the night is not good for me. Every day from 11 to 1 o'clock I have classes in my rooms and I talk [to] them till they [grow] tired. The Brooklyn course ended yesterday. Another lecture I have there next Monday.

Bean soup and rice or barley is now my general diet. I am faring well. Financially I am making the ends meet and nothing more because I do not charge anything for the classes I have in my rooms. And the public lectures have to go through so many hands.

I have a good many lectures planned ahead in New York, which I hope to deliver by and by. Sister Isabel wrote to me a beautiful letter and she does so much for me. My eternal gratitude to her.

Baby has stopped writing; I do not know why

Kindly tell Baby to send me a little Sanskrit book which came from India. I forgot to bring it over. I want to translate some passages from it.

Mr. [Charles M.] Higgins is full of joy. It was he who planned all this for me, and he is so glad that everything succeeded so well.

Mrs. Guernsey is going to give up this house and going to some other house. Miss [Florence] Guernsey wants to marry but her father and mother do not like it at all. I am very sorry for her, poor "Sister Jenny" — and so many men are after her. Here is a very rich railway gentleman called Mr. [Austin] Corbin; his only daughter, Miss [Anna] Corbin, is very much interested in me. And though she is one of the leaders of the 400, she is very intellectual and spiritual too, in a way. Their house is always chock full of swells and foreign aristocracy. Princes and Barons and whatnot from all over the world. Some of these foreigners are very bright. I am sorry your home-manufactured aristocracy is not very interesting. Behind her parlor she has a long arbour with all sorts of palms and seats and electric light. There I will have a little class next week of a score of long-pockets. The Fun is not bad. "This world is a great humbug after all", Mother. "God alone is real; everything else is a dream only." Mother Temple says she does not like to be bossed by you and that is why she does not come to Chicago. She is very happy nearby. Between swells and Delmonico and Waldorf dinners, my health was going to be injured. So I quickly turned a thorough vegetarian to avoid all invitations. The rich are really the salt of this world — they are neither food nor drink. Goodbye for the present.

Your ever affectionate Son,

VIVEKANANDA

L

To Mrs. G. W. Hale

54 W. 33RD ST., NEW YORK

11 March 1895

DEAR MOTHER,

Many thanks for your kind letter. I will be only too glad to have an orange coat, provided it be light as summer is approaching.

I do not remember whether the Cook's letters of credit I have are limited as to their time or not. It is high time we look into them. If they are limited, don't you think it is better to put them in some bank? I have about a thousand dollars in the Boston bank and a few hundred in the New York — they all go to India by this week or next. So it is better that I look into the Cook's letters, and it will be foolish to get into trouble by having them past the date.

There are a few more Sanskrit books which have not been sent — one pretty thick and broad, the other two very thin. Kindly send them as soon as you can.

Mrs. [Milward] Adams, Mrs. [Ole] Bull, and Miss Emma Thursby are gone to Chicago today.

With eternal love to the babies and to you and Father Pope.

I remain ever your affectionate Son,

VIVEKANANDA

LI

To Mrs. G. W. Hale

[54 W. 33RD ST., NEW YORK]

14 March 1895

DEAR MOTHER,

The last letter you sent over is a notice from the Chicago post office of a parcel received by them. I think it is some books sent to me from India. The rugs cannot come through the post office (?) I do not know what to do. I send you therefore back this notice, and if they deliver it to you, all right — else I hope you will ask them to send it over to New York and kindly give them my address.

Yours obediently,

VIVEKANANDA

LII

To Mrs. G. W. Hale

[NEW YORK

April 25, 1895]

DEAR MOTHER,

I was away a long time in the country. Came back day before yesterday.

I think the summer coat is in Chicago. If so, will you kindly send it over c/o Miss Phillips, 19 W. 38 Str., New York? It is getting hot here every day.

I will remain in New York till the end of May, at least.

Hoping you are all in perfect health. I remain yours truly,

VIVEKANANDA

LIII

To Mrs. G. W. Hale

54 W. 33.

NEW YORK

[April 26, 1895]

DEAR MOTHER,

Perhaps you did not receive my letter asking you to send the Calcutta pamphlets about the Paramahamsa Ramakrishna. Kindly send them to me at 54 W. 33, and also the pamphlets about the Calcutta meeting if you have any. Also the summer coat to the care of Miss Phillips, 19 W. 38.

As I do not see any probability of my going soon to Chicago, I am thinking of drawing all my money from the Chicago bank to New York. Will you kindly ascertain the exact total amount I have in Chicago so that I may draw it out at once and deposit it in some New York bank?

Kindly do these and I will bother you no more. I have written to India long ago about the rugs. I do not know whether Dewanji is alive or dead. I have no information.

I am all right and will be more than a month yet in New York. After that I am going to the Thousand Islands — wherever that place may be — for a little summer quiet and rest. Mrs. Bagley has been down here to see me and attended several of my classes.

The classes are going on with a boom; almost every day I have one, and they are packed full. But no *"money"* — except they maintain themselves. I charge no fees, except as the members contribute to the rent etc. voluntarily.

It is mostly probable that I will go away this summer.

With my love to all,

Ever gratefully yours,

VIVEKANANDA

LIV

To Mrs. G. W. Hale

54 W. 33 NEW YORK

The 1st of May 1895

DEAR MOTHER,

Many, many thanks for sending the coat. Now I am well equipped for summer. I am so sorry the rugs could not come before I leave this country. They will come if Dewanji is alive.

I have been out of town a few days and have now come back all right — healthy as ever.

Lord bless you ever and ever for your untiring kindness to me.

Ever your grateful Son,

VIVEKANANDA

P.S. *The History of Rajasthan* I present you, and the satchel to the babies. Yours,

VIVEKANANDA

LV

To Mr. Francis H. Leggett

54 W. 33RD ST.

NEW YORK

THE 4TH MAY '95

DEAR FRIEND,

Many thanks for your kind present. The cigars are indeed delicious — and a hundred times so, as coming from you.

With everlasting love and regards,

I remain yours truly,

VIVEKANANDA

LVI

To Mrs. G. W. Hale

54 W. 33

NEW YORK

16th May '95

DEAR MOTHER,

Your kind note duly reached. The books have arrived safe and more are coming. The Sanskrit books pay no duty, being classics. I expect a big package from Khetri. The big packet was from the Raja of Khetri, sending me an address from a meeting held of Rajput nobility at Mount Abu, for my work in this country.

I do not know whether I will be able to come over to Chicago or not. I am trying to get a free pass; in case I succeed I will come, else not. Financially this winter's work was no success at all — I could barely keep myself up — but spiritually very great. I am going to the Thousand Islands for the summer to visit a friend and some of my pupils will be there.

I have got plenty of books now to read from India, and I will be quite engaged this summer.

The Khetri package will not arrive soon, so kindly make arrangements that it will be received during your absence if you go away. [There] will have to be paid a heavy duty for [it,] I am afraid.

Mrs. [Florence] Adams brought me the love from the [Hale] Sisters on her way to Europe. She started this morning. A large package of books also I expect soon. The original Upanishads — there is no duty on them.

I have had some trouble with my stomach; hope it will be over in a few days.

With love to all, I am ever your affectionate Son,

VIVEKANANDA

LVII

To Mrs. Ole Bull

NEW YORK

The 28th May '95

DEAR MOTHER,

Your last kind letter to hand. This week will be the last of my classes. I am going next Tuesday with Mr. Leggett to Maine. He has a fine lake and a forest there. I will be two or three weeks there. Thence I go to the Thousand Islands. Also I have an invitation to speak at a parliament of religions at Toronto, Canada, on July 18th. I will go there from Thousand Islands and return back.

So far everything is going on well with me.

Ever your grateful son,

VIVEKANANDA

P.S. My regards and love to your daughter and pray for her speedy recovery.

LVIII

To Dr. Paul Carus

19 W. 38TH ST.,

NEW YORK

June [May] 28, '95

DR. PAUL CARUS, LA SALLE, ILL.

DEAR SIR,

I am just now in receipt of your letter and will be very happy to join the religions Congress at Toronto. Only, as you are well aware of, the financial means of a "Bhikshu" (A Hindu or Buddhist monk.) are very limited. I will be only too glad to do anything in my power to help you and wait further particulars and directions.

Hoping to hear from you soon and thanking you very much for your great sympathy with Buddhistic India.

I remain ever fraternally your,

VIVEKANANDA

LIX

Mrs. Ole Bull

4th June '95

DEAR MOTHER

Today I leave New York at 5 p.m. by steamer with Mr. Leggett.

The classes were closed on Saturday last [June 1] and so far the work has been very successful, no small part of which is due to you.

Ever praying for you and yours,

I am ever your faithful Son,

VIVEKANANDA

P.S. I will acquaint you with my whereabouts as soon as I know it myself.

LX

To Dr. Paul Carus

C/O MISS DUTCHER

THOUSAND ISLAND PARK

N. Y.

[June 1895]

DEAR DOCTOR,

I am in this place now and had to change some of my plans on account of the Toronto Congress.

I am therefore not quite sure whether I will be able to come to Oak Island Conference. It is very possible, however, that I will be able to do so.

I also hope Mr. [Charles Carroll] Bonney will come. He is a noble, noble soul — one who sincerely wishes the fellowship of all humanity.

Is it not true, Dr., that Mr. Bonney, as I have every reason to think, originated the plan of the parliament of religions?

I will certainly try my best to come.

Thanking you very much for your kindness, I remain

Ever yours in the Lord of Compassion,

VIVEKANANDA

P.S. Will you kindly inform me what lines of thought you want me to take.

LXI

To Mrs. G. W. Hale

C/O MISS DUTCHER'S

THOUSAND ISLAND PARK

N. Y.

2nd July 1895

DEAR MOTHER —

You did not write to me a single line for a long time. Neither did Sister Mary write about the duty paid on the rugs [from the Dewan of Junagadh]. I am afraid the rugs are small.

Here is another consignment from Raja Ajit Singh [the Maharaja of Khetri] consisting of carpets, shawls, etc., etc., for which the bill of lading you sent me the other day. This consignment has no *duty* to pay because it was all prepaid in India, and the bill of lading says so expressly. I will send you the bill of lading and the receipt for the *duty*. Kindly take one more trouble for me and get it out of the express company. And keep it with you till I come. The goods have arrived in New York and I had a notice of that. They are on their way to Chicago.

In two or three days I will send the bill of lading and the receipt for duty paid, to you. I foolishly asked Miss Phillips, as soon as I got the Company's (Original letter: Companies'.) notice, to get them out before I got the bill of lading. Now the bill of lading shows that it is bound for Chicago. So I am bound to give you this trouble. I am so sorry. Again with my usual business instincts — I forgot to note down the name of the express company. So I have written to New York for the letters of the Company. As soon as that comes I will send over to you.

I am going to Europe by the end of August or a little later.

I will come to see you by the end of August.

Lord bless you and yours for ever and ever.

Your ever affectionate Son,

VIVEKANANDA

LXII

To Mrs. G. W. Hale

THOUSAND ISLAND PARK, N.Y.

C/O MISS DUTCHER

July 3, 1895

DEAR MOTHER –

Herewith I send you the bill of landing and the inventory of the goods sent from India. The duty, as you will find, has been prepaid, so there is no botheration on that score. The goods have reached Hull. They will be here by the middle of this month. And if you see a letter with the Morris American Express Co. name on the envelope, tear it open. You need not forward it to me, for that will be the notice of arrival to Chicago. I am sure Dewanji's carpets were too small, but why do you not write to me about the duty if you had to pay it? I insist upon paying it myself. The Raja's things seem to come very quick. I am so glad too I will have something to present to Mrs. Bagley, Mrs. Bull, etc.

[Enclosed in the above letter was the following note.]

541 DEARBORN AVE.

CHICAGO.

TO THE MORRIS EXPRESS CO.–

DEAR SIR,

Please permit Mrs. G. W. Hale of 541 Dearborn Ave., Chicago, to act for me about the goods sent to me from India and receive the same.

I have the honor to be, sir, your most obedient servant,

SWAMI VIVEKANANDA

LXIII

To Mrs. Ole Bull

C/O MISS DUTCHER

THOUSAND ISLAND PARK

N. Y.

13th [postmarked 11th] July '95.

DEAR MOTHER,

The shirts arrived yesterday; they are nice and fit me well.

Everybody liked them.

Landsberg arrived this morning with a picture of Shri Ramakrishna.

The Toronto affair has fallen through because the clergyman objected to a heathen. There is one invitation from the Christian Union of Oak Beach. I do not know whether I will go there.

As I intend to go to Chicago, in August, I ought to give to the people here all the time I can.

I do not know yet the exact date when I start [for Europe] — but somewhere at the end of August, I am sure.

Landsberg sends his love to all the rest.

Ever yours in love and gratitude,

VIVEKANANDA

LXIV

To Mrs. G. W. Hale

THOUSAND ISLAND PARK

C/O MISS DUTCHER

N. Y.

27th July '95

DEAR MOTHER –

I will be ever so much obliged if you kindly look into the "bead" affair. (Rudrâksha beads sent from India. Vide letter dated January 17, 1895 in Complete Works, VI.) I think there will be a little duty to pay. I will pay it to you when I come.

I start from here next week. I will be in Detroit a day or two on my way. I will be in by the third or fourth of August.

With Everlasting love, your Son,

VIVEKANANDA

[Enclosed in the above letter was the following note.]

27th July '95

TO THE UNITED STATES EXPRESS COMPANY

FOREIGN DEPARTMENT.

DEAR SIR,

Herewith I authorize Mrs. George W. Hale to take delivery of the "beads" that have been expressed to me from India. Hoping they will be regularly delivered to her, I remain yours obediently,

SWAMI VIVEKANANDA

LXV

To Mrs. G. W. Hale

C/O MISS DUTCHER

THOUSAND ISLAND PARK

30th August [July] '95

DEAR MOTHER,

I was starting for Chicago, Thursday next [August 1], but your letter stopped me. The letter and the package have safely arrived.

Write to me or wire if you want me to come to Chicago. I will then start for Chicago next week, i.e. on Tuesday next [August 6]. I thought Sister Mary was at home. When are the other babies coming? My going to Europe is not yet settled finally. The babies have not written me a line — not one of them.

Oh, Mother, my heart is so, so sad. The letters bring the news of the death of Dewanji. Haridas Viharidas has left the body. He was as a father to me. Poor man, he was the last 5 years seeking the retirement from business life, and at last he got it but could not enjoy it long. I pray that he may never come back again to this dirty hole they call the Earth. Neither may he be born in heaven or any other horrid place. May he never again wear a body — good or bad, thick or thin. What a humbug and illusion this world is, Mother, what a mockery this life. I pray constantly that all mankind will come to know the reality, i.e. God, and this "Shop" here be closed for ever.

My heart is too full to write more. Write to me or wire if you like.

Your ever obedient Son,

VIVEKANANDA

P.S. We will think of the coming package [from the Maharaja of Khetri] in Chicago. How long will you be in Chicago? If it is only a week or so, I need not come. I will meet you in New York. If more than that, I come to see you.

Yours,

LXVI

To Mrs. G. W. Hale

C/O MISS DUTCHER

THOUSAND ISLAND PARK

N. Y.

[July 31, 1895]

DEAR MOTHER –

I am afraid I can not come to see you and neither will you advise me. I am going with a friend (Mr. Francis Leggett.) to Europe, at his expense. We go first to Paris and from there to London. My friend will go to Italy and I to London. I will, however, come back to New York in *September*. So I am not going away for good.

I start on the 17th. So you see, it is impossible to come and go that way for 3 or 4 days.

The package from India ought to have reached by this time. If they come, (The goods mentioned in Swami Vivekananda's letter dated July 2, 1895.) kindly take the delivery and send it back to New York to Miss Mary Phillips, 19 W. 38. If the package does not come to Chicago before you go away, then kindly send the bill of lading etc. to Miss Mary Phillips, 19. W. 38. The babies [the Hale daughters] did not write me a line, nor did they intimate where they are. I absolutely do not know anything about them. As they do not want it, it seems I ought not to disturb them with my letters. But you kindly convey them my love and eternal, undying blessings. So to you, Mother and Father Pope. I will pen a longer epistle in a few days. We will see each other next spring in Chicago, Mother, if we all live.

Ever gratefully your Son,

VIVEKANANDA

LXVII

To Mr. Francis Leggett

[THOUSAND ISLAND PARK, U.S.A.

August 1895]

DEAR FRIEND,

I received your note duly.

Very kind of you and noble to ask me to have my own time to London. Many thanks for that. But I am in no hurry for London and, moreover, *I want to see you married in Paris* and then I go over to London.

I will be ready, Father Leggett, at hand and in time — never fear.

Yours affectionately ever,

VIVEKANANDA

LXVIII

To Mrs. G. W. Hale

THE WESTERN UNION TELEGRAPH COMPANY.

RECEIVED AT: PLAZA HOTEL DRUG STORE,

NORTH AVE. & CLARK STREET.

THOUSAND ISLAND, N.Y., 2, '95

[August 2, 1895]

8 jw ws 11 paid 1.33 p.m.

MRS. G. W. HALE

541 DEARBORN AVE.

WHY ANY CHARGES DUTY PREPAID (This evidently again refers to the goods sent by the Maharaja of Khetri. *Vide* the letter addressed to Mrs. G. W. Hale dated July 2, 1895.) YOU HAVE DOCUMENTS WRITE FULL PARTICULARS.

VIVEKANANDA

LXIX

To Sister Christine

19 WEST 38TH STREET

9th August '95

DEAR CHRISTINA,

You must be enjoying the beautiful weather very much. Here, it is extremely hot but it does not worry me much. I had a pleasant journey from Thousand Islands to New York; and though the Engine was derailed, I did not know anything of it, being asleep all the time. Miss Waldo went out of the train at Albany. I did not see her off as I was asleep. I have not heard anything from her yet. Hope to hear soon. Dr. [L. L. Wight] and Miss [Ruth] Ellis must have gone home by this time.

We gave them a telepathic message but Miss Ellis has not got it sure, else she would write.

I am making preparations for my departure.

I came in time for one of the meetings here and had another one last evening — going to have one more this evening and almost every evening till I go over.

What is Mrs. Funkey [Mary Caroline Funke] doing, and Miss [Mary Elizabeth] Dutcher? Do you go to meditate on the mountain as usual? Did you hear from Kripananda?

Write to me as soon as you can — I am so anxious to hear from you.

Ever yours with blessings and love,

VIVEKANANDA

P.S. My love and blessings to Mrs. Funkey and Miss Dutcher.

LXX

To Mrs. Ole Bull

19 WEST 38TH STREET

NEW YORK

9th August '95

DEAR MOTHER –

Your note duly received. I saw also Miss Thursby yesterday. After the *hard work* at the Thousand Islands, I am taking a few days quiet and preparation for my departure. So I cannot come to Greenacre. I am with Miss Phillips and will be till the 17th, on which day I depart for Europe. I have seen Mr. Leggett. You remember Mrs. Sturges, the widow in black in my classes. She is going to marry Mr. Leggett in Paris. They will be married the 1st week we arrive, and then they go on a tour through Europe, and I, to England. I hope to return in a few weeks – back to New York.

Kindly give to Miss Hamlin [Elizabeth L. Hamlen], to Miss [Sarah] Farmer, Dr. [L. L. Wight] and Miss Howe, and all our friends my greetings, love and good-bye.

Ever sincerely your Son,

VIVEKANANDA

LXXI

To Sister Christine

[The following telegram was sent on Swami Vivekananda's behalf.]

POSTAL TELEGRAPH-CABLE COMPANY

RECEIVED AT MAIN OFFICE, COR. GRISWOLD

LAFAYETTE AVE., DETROIT, MICH.

43. NY. FC. W. . . 10 PAID. 12:45 PM

NEW YORK, N.Y.

[August 17, 1895]

MISS CHRISTINA GREENSTIDEL,

418 ALFRED ST., DETROIT, MICH.

SWAMM [SWAMI] LEAVING SENDS YOU AND MRS. FUNKE LOVE AND BLESSING.

KRIPANANDA.

LXXII

To Miss Isabelle McKindley

80 OAKLEY STREET

CHELSEA, S.W.

LONDON.

24th October '95

We meet and part. This is the law and ever ever be.
I sadly ask O gentle ones Do you remember me?

I haven't had any news from Chicago, nor did I write as I did not want to bother you — also I did not know where to.

Accompanying is a newspaper notice of a lecture I delivered in London. It is not bad. The London audiences are very learned and critical, and the English nature is far from being effusive. I have some friends here — made some more — so I am going on.

My bed is in the foaming deep
What care I, friend, the dew!

It is a queer life, mine — always travelling, no rest. Rest will be my death — such is the force of habit. Little success here, little there — and a good deal of bumping. Saw Paris a good [deal]. Miss Josephine M'cLeod [MacLeod], a New York friend, showed it all over to me for a month. Even there, the kind American girl! Here in England they know us more. Those that do not like the Hindus, they hate them; those that like, they worship them.

It is slow work here, but sure. Not frothy, not superficial. English women as a rule are not as highly educated as the American women, nor are so beautiful. They are quite submissive wives or hidden-away daughters or church-going mothers — the embodiments of crystallized conventionality. I am going to have some classes at the above address.

Sometimes — and generally when I score a success — I feel a despondence; I feel as if everything is vain — as if this life has no meaning, as if it is a waking dream. Love, friendship, religion, virtue, kindness — everything, a momentary state of mind. I seem to long to go; in spite of myself I say, how far — O how far! Yet the body-and-mind will have to work its *Karma* out. I hope it will not be bad.

How are you all going on? Where is Mother Church? Is she interviewing the ghosts of the Thotmeses and Rameses in the Pyramids — or calmly going her round of duties at home?

Yet the life seems to grow deep and at the same time lose its hold on itself.

Not disgust, nor joy for life, but a sort of indifference — things will take their course; who can resist — only stand by and look on. Well, I will not talk about myself so much. Egregious egotist! I always was that, you know. How about you all? Great fun this life, isn't it? Don't go to the extremes. A calm, restful, settled married life is good for the majority of mankind. Mr. [Edward T.] Sturdy, the friend with whom I am living now, was in India several times. He mixed with our monks and is very ascetic in his habits, but he is married at last and has settled down. And [he] has got a beautiful little baby. Their life is very nice. The wife, of course, doesn't much care about metaphysics or Sanskrit, but her whole life is in her husband — and husband's soul is in Sanskrit metaphysics! Yet it is a good combination of theory and practice, I think. Write me all about yourselves if you have time and inclination, and give Mother Church my eternal gratitude.

My movements are so, so uncertain. Yet I will be a month more in London.

With never-ending gratitude and love,

VIVEKANANDA

LXXIII

To Sister Christine

228 W. 39TH STREET

[NEW YORK]

8th Dec. '95

DEAR CHRISTINA,

I am once more on American Soil and have taken lodgings at 228 W. 39, where I begin work from Monday next. Sometime after Christmas I intend to make a tour through Detroit and Chicago.

I do not care for public lecturings at all — and do not think I shall have any more public lectures charging admission. If you will see Mrs. Phelps and others of our friends and arrange some classes (strictly on nonpayment basis), it will facilitate things a good deal.

Write at your earliest opportunity and give Mrs. Phunkey [Funke] and all our friends my deepest love and gratitude.

Yours ever in the Lord,

VIVEKANANDA

P.S. Kripananda is over full of praise of you and Mrs. Funkey [Funke] and sends his loving regards for you.

LXXIV

To Sister Christine

228 W. 39TH STREET

[NEW YORK

Dec. 10, 1895

D CHRISTINA,

Perhaps by this time you have received my first letter. I received yours just now.

I had a splendid success in England and have left a *nucleus* there to work till my arrival next summer. You will be astonished to learn that some of my strongest friends are big "guns" of the Church of England.

This Christmas I am going away a week, from 24th Decem., to the country with Mr. and Mrs. Leggett — after that I resume my work. In the meanwhile the classes have begun.

I have written to you my intention of taking a quick turn through Detroit and Chicago in the meanwhile and [then] return back.

Give Mrs. Phelps my love and kindly arrange the classes [in Detroit] with her. The best thing is to arrange for a public lecture where I give out my general plan of work. The Unitarian church is available; and if the lecture is free, there will be a big crowd. The collection most possibly will cover the expenses. Then out of this we will get the materials of a big class and then hurry them through, leaving Mrs. Phelps and you and Mrs. Funkey [Funke] to work on with them.

This plan is entirely feasible and if Mrs. Phelps and Mrs. Bagley desire it, they can work it out very quickly.

Ever yours with love and blessings,

VIVEKANANDA

LXXV

To Sister Christine

228 W. 39TH STREET

NEW YORK

12 December 1895

DEAR CHRISTINA,

I am going away out of town from the 24th of this month and will come back on the 2nd of January. From the 24th — the 2nd I will not be here. I will settle the dates for Detroit and Chicago after hearing from you and from Chicago.

[Paragraph excised from the original letter.]

My love to Mrs. Phunkey [Funke] [excised] and all other friends.

Ever yours in the Lord,

VIVEKANANDA

LXXVI

To the Maharaja of Limdi,

Cathiawad, Bombay

CHICAGO

14th Dec. '95

YOUR HIGHNESS,

The gentleman whom I have the pleasure of introducing to you was the chairman of the Parliament of Religions held in Chicago.

He is a holy and noble gentleman. We owe him a deep debt of gratitude; and as he is going to make a tour through India, I hope your Highness will extend him the same hospitality as he has to us.

Yours with blessings,

VIVEKANANDA

LXXVII

To the Dewan of Mysore, Madras (His Excellency Seshahari Iyer, K. C. S. I.)

CHICAGO,

the 14th Dec. '95

DEAR SIR –

The gentleman I have the pleasure of introducing to you was the chairman of the Chicago Parliament of religions.

All India owes him a deep debt of gratitude. He is now on a tour through our country, and I am sure you will help him in seeing your part of the country and oblige.

Yours with blessings,

VIVEKANANDA

LXXVIII

To Sister Christine

228 W. 39TH STREET

NEW YORK

December 24, 1895

DEAR CHRISTINA —

Merry Christmas and happy New Year to you. I am going today to the country. I return in 10 days.

About the tour through Detroit — I will fix it later on. I am afraid if I go just now, everything here will fall to pieces.

I will come anyway, but I am afraid it will be later than I expected.

My love to Mrs. Phelps, Mrs. Phunkey [Funke] and all our friends and Christmas greetings.

Ever yours in the Lord,

VIVEKANANDA

P.S. Kripananda sends his greetings too.

LXXIX

To Mrs. Ole Bull

228 W. 39

NEW YORK

24 December 1895

Merry Christmas and happy New Year to you, dear Mrs. Bull. And may peace and health rest on you and yours for ever. I am going out of town today and will be back in ten days.

My love to all.

Yours affectionately,

VIVEKANANDA

LXXX

To the Editor of Light of the East

1896.

DEAR SIR,

Many thanks for your kindly sending me several copies of the *Light of the East*. I wish the paper all success.

As you have asked for my suggestion [that] I can make towards improving the paper — I must frankly state that in my life-long experience in the work, I have always found "Occultism" injurious and weakening to humanity. What we want is strength. We Indians, more than any other race, want strong and vigorous thought. We have enough of the superfine in all concerns. For centuries we have been stuffed with the mysterious; the result is that our intellectual and spiritual digestion is almost hopelessly impaired, and the race has been dragged down to the depths of hopeless imbecility — never before or since experienced by any other civilised community. There must be freshness and vigour of thought behind to make a virile race. More than enough to strengthen the whole world exists in the Upanishads. The Advaita is the eternal mine of strength. But it requires to be *applied*. It must first be cleared of the incrustation of scholasticism, and then in all its simplicity, beauty and sublimity be taught over the length and breadth of the land, as applied even to the minutest detail of daily life. "This is a very large order"; but we must work towards it, nevertheless, as if it would be accomplished to-morrow. Of one thing I am sure — that whoever wants to help his fellow beings through genuine love and unselfishness will work wonders.

Yours truly,

VIVEKANANDA

LXXXI

To Mrs. Ole Bull

228 W. 39TH STREET

NEW YORK

the 3rd Jan. '96

DEAR MRS. BULL—

I have had a letter from Mr. Trine asking me to have some classes at the Procopeia in February. I do not see my way to go to Boston in February, however I may like it. I have given up for the present my plan of going to Detroit and Chicago in February. Later on I will try. Miss [Josephine] Locke will see to my having classes in Chicago and I have some friends in Detroit I may go to Baltimore for a few days in the meanwhile. I enjoyed my visit with the Leggetts exceedingly. It has braced me for further work. I am very well both physically and mentally.

Wishing you a happy New Year,

I remain yours affectionately,

VIVEKANANDA

LXXXII

To Mrs. Charles (Mary) Funke

228 W. 39

NEW YORK,

the 6th Jan. 1896.

DEAR MRS. FUNKEY [FUNKE] —

Many, many thanks for the sweet flowers. It recalls to me the beautiful times we had at the Thousand Islands and presages many such summer gatherings.

The work here had begun in right earnest, and we will advance it farther this year than in the last.

I am therefore uncertain as to the exact date of my coming to Detroit. I will come, however, very soon.

Yours ever in the Lord,

VIVEKANANDA

LXXXIII

To Mrs. Ole Bull

228 W. 39TH STREET

NEW YORK

10 January 1896

DEAR MRS. BULL,

I have received your letter and also another from the Secretary of the Harvard Metaphysical Club.

I will be only too glad to come to Boston for the Harvard lecture especially — but these are the difficulties in the way: First, the work here will fall to pieces; secondly, I have begun to write in right earnest. I want to finish some text books to be the basis of work when I am gone. I want to hurry through four little text books before I go.

Of course it is impossible to come this month as the notices of the four Sunday lectures are out. In the first week of February I have again a lecture at Brooklyn at Dr. Janes's. My idea now is to make a tour to Boston, Detroit, and Chicago in March and then come back to New York a week or so and then start for England. In March I will be able to stay a few weeks at each of these places. Of course it is true that [as] yet I have no competent persons here to carry on the work like Sturdy in England, nor any sincere friend to stand by me except you.

I will do anything you want me to, and if you think it is good for me to come to Boston in February, I am ready.

Ever yours with gratitude, love, and blessings

VIVEKANANDA

P.S. I have not much faith in that Procopeia business, (The Procopeia Club.) except as a nucleus to work from.

My love to Miss Hamlin and all the other friends there.

YOURS, V.

LXXXIV

To Sister Christine

24th Jan. '95 ['96]

DEAR CHRISTINA,

I have not heard from you [for] long. Hope everything is going on well with you and Mrs. Phunkey [Funke].

Did you receive my poem? I had a letter from Mrs. Phelps today. I am coming to Detroit next March early, as I will have to finish my February course in New York. The public lectures will be printed as they are delivered right along. The class lectures will very soon be collected and edited in little volumes.

May the Lord bless you ever and ever.

Yours ever with love and blessings,

VIVEKANANDA

LXXXV

To Mrs. Ole Bull

228 W. 39

NEW YORK

the 6th of Feb. '96

DEAR MRS. BULL —

I received your last duly, but owing to many things I have given up the idea of taking rest next month. I go to Detroit the first week of March and then, towards the middle or last week, come to Boston. I have not much faith in working such things as the Procopeia [Club] etc.— because these mixed-up conglomerations of all isms and ities — mostly fads — disturb the steadiness of the mind, and life becomes a mass of frivolities. I am very glad, however, to get an opportunity to talk to the graduates of Harvard. This does not mean that I am not coming to Procopeia. I will come but it will be only for your sake. There is one if, however — and that is if I am physically able. My health has nearly broken down. I have not slept even one night soundly in New York since I came; and this year there is incessant work, both with the pen and the mouth. The accumulated work and worry of years is on me now, I am afraid. Then a big struggle awaits me in England. I wish to go to the bottom of the sea and have a good, long sleep.

To Detroit I must go, dead or alive, as I have disappointed them several times last year. There were big money offers from near Chicago. I have rejected them as I do not any longer believe in paid lectures and their utility in any country. If after Detroit I feel the body able to drag itself on to Boston, I will come, else I will remain in Detroit or some other quiet place and rest to recuperate for the coming work in England. So far I have tried to work conscientiously — let the fruits belong to the Lord. If they were good they will sprout up sooner or later; if bad, the sooner they die the better. I am quite satisfied with my task in life. I have been much more active than a Sannyasin ought to be. Now I will disappear from society altogether. The touch of the world is degenerating me, I am sure, so it is time to be off. Work has no more value beyond purifying the heart. My heart is pure enough; why shall I bother my head about doing good to others? "If you have known the Atman as the one, only existence and nothing else exists, desiring what? — for whose desire you trouble yourself?" This universe is a dream, pure and simple. Why bother myself about a dream? The very atmosphere of the world is poison to the Yogi, but I am waking up. My old iron heart is coming back — all attachments of relatives, friends, disciples are vanishing fast. "Neither through wealth nor through progeny, but by giving up everything as chaff is that immortality attained" — the Vedas. I am so tired of talking too; I want to close my lips and sit in silence for years. All talk is nonsense.

Yours faithfully,

VIVEKANANDA

LXXXVI

To Miss Emma Thursby

228 W. 39TH STREET

NEW YORK,

February 26th, 1896

DEAR MISS THURSBY,

Will you oblige me by giving Mr. Goodwin any particulars you can with reference to the business arrangements made for my 6 lectures with Miss Corbin. He will see her, with the idea of obtaining payment.

Thanking you in anticipation, and with best regards,

Very truly yours,

VIVEKANANDA

LXXXVII

To Shri Giridharidas Mangaldas Viharidas Desai

228 W. 39TH STREET

NEW YORK

2 March 1896

DEAR FRIEND,

Excuse my delay in replying to your beautiful note.

Your uncle was a great soul, and his whole life was given to doing good to his country. Hope you will all follow in his footsteps.

I am coming to India this winter, and cannot express my sorrow that I will not see Haribhai once more.

He was a strong, noble friend, and India has lost a good deal in losing him.

I am going to England very soon where I intend to pass the summer, and in winter next I come to India.

Recommend me to your uncles and friends.

Ever always the well-wisher of your family,

VIVEKANANDA

PS: My England address is: C/o E. T. Sturdy, Esq., High View, Caversham, Reading, England.

LXXXVIII

To Sister Christine

C/O THE PROCOPEIA

45 ST., BOTOLPH STREET

BOSTON, MASS.

22nd March '96

DEAR CHRISTINA,

Herewith [words excised] to countersign it and put it [words excised]. I am afraid I have made a mistake in writing Miss to your name. In that case you will have to sign also as Miss etc.

I am enjoying Boston very much, especially the old friends here.

They are all kind. Reply promptly. Write fully later on.

With everlasting love and blessings,

Yours etc.,

VIVEKANANDA

LXXXIX

To Mrs. Charles (Mary) Funke

C/O THE PROCOPEIA

45 ST., BOTOLPH STREET

BOSTON, MASS.

22nd March '96

DEAR MRS. FUNKEY [FUNKE] –

I had no time to write a line even, I was so busy. I am enjoying Boston immensely, only hard work. The meeting with old friends is very pleasing, no doubt. The so-called class swelled up to 500 people last night and, am afraid, will go on increasing. Everything going on splendidly. Mr. Goodwin as nice as ever. We are all friends here. I go next week to Chicago.

Hope everything is going on well with you there. Kindly give my love to Mrs. Phelps, Mr. Phelps and all the rest of my friends.

With all love and blessings,

Yours,

VIVEKANANDA

XC

To Sister Christine

1628 INDIANA AVE.

CHICAGO, ILL.

[April 6, 1896]

DEAR CHRISTINA,

[Line excised.] reply as soon as possible.

I am going forward to New York on Thursday [April 9] and [will] start for England on the 15th of April.

Goodby and love to you all — to Mrs. Funkey [Funke], to Mrs. Phelps and all the rest of our friends.

In this life we meet and part again and again; but the mind is omnipresent and can be, hear, and feel anywhere.

Yours with love and blessings,

VIVEKANANDA

P.S. Give Kripananda and Miss [Martha] Hamilton my love and blessings when you meet them next.

[Written in the margin:] I will go to New York next Friday [April 10].

XCI

To Sister Christine

HIGH VIEW, CAVERSHAM

READING, LONDON.

26th April '96

DEAR CHRISTINA,

How are things going on with you? I am all safe and sound here in England. Going to begin work from May fourth. How is Mrs. Funkey [Funke]?

Give them all my Love. Write me all about yourself and Mrs. Funkey when you have time. Address me at 63 St., George's Road, S.W. London.

Where is Krip. [Swami Kripananda]? What is he doing now? Has he been able to get up any classes yet? Has his temper gone down?

Give them all my love — and [to] Miss Hamilton and to all my friends and to the Rabbi [Grossman of Detroit].

Yours ever with love and blessings,

VIVEKANANDA

XCII

To Mrs. Ole Bull

63 ST GEORGE'S ROAD
LONDON. S.W.
May 8, 1896
DEAR MRS. BULL —

Your last letter to Sturdy at hand. They, I am sorry to say, leave us nowhere. I could not make anything out of them.

What are we to do? Is the book going to be published or not? Prof. [William] James's introduction (Preface to Swami Vivekananda's Râja-Yoga.) is of no use in England. So why wait so long for that; and what use are those long explanations about him?

Our hands are tied down. Why do you not write something plain and decisive? Life is short and time is flying. I am so sorry you are losing sight of that. Your letters are full of explanations [and] directions, but not one word *about what is to be done*!!! So much red tape about printing a little book!! Empires are managed with less manipulation than that, I am sure!! So kindly write at your earliest something precise about the book and whether it is going to be printed or not, and pray make the writing a little legible.

Poor Sturdy is out of his wits as to what to do; he has gone through the Mss. long ago.

Joking apart, I am very sorry you are not coming over this year. We are in Lady Isabel's house. (The house was rented from Lady Isabel Margesson.) Miss [Henrietta] Müller has taken some rooms in it too. Goodwin is here with us. We have not yet made any big stir here. The classes have begun; they are not yet what we expected. We [have] had only two yet.

We will work on steadily the next 4 or 5 months. Sturdy is as patient and persevering and hopeful as ever.

It is cool enough here yet to have a fire in the grate.

Give my love to Mrs. Adams, Miss Thursby and all other friends. My love to Mr. Fox and blessings.

Yours with love and blessings,

VIVEKANANDA

XCIII

To Mr. Francis Leggett

(Swami Vivekananda enclosed the following document in a July 6, 1896 letter written to Francis Leggett.)

63 ST. GEORGE'S ROAD, LONDON, S.W.

6th July 1896

TO FRANCIS LEGGETT, ESQ.

DEAR SIR,

Herewith I constitute you as my attorney and representative in regards to all publication pamphlets etc., written or dictated by me, their copyright, sale, etc., in the U.S. of America.

Yours affectionately,

VIVEKANANDA

XCIV

To Mrs. Ole Bull

63 ST. GEORGE'S ROAD, LONDON, S.W.

6th July 1896

DEAR MRS. BULL —

I have sent to Mr. Leggett by last mail the power of attorney, and, as you desired, this is to notify you of the fact and absolve you from the responsibilities of the power of attorney which I gave you in America last year.

Yours affectionately,

VIVEKANANDA

Saradananda and Goodwin have arrived, I am sure, by this time. I have a nice letter from Dr. Jain [Dr. Lewis G. Janes]. I am going to Switzerland for a vacation in a few days. I mean to stay there a month or more. I will return to London in the next fall. I do not know when I go back to India.

Things are growing nicely here.

With love to all,

Yours affectionately,

XCV

To Mrs. G. W. Hale

July 7, 1896

DEAR MOTHER –

[On the] 18th of this month I start for Switzerland for a holiday. I will come back to London again to work in the Autumn. The work in England bids fair to be much better and deeper than in the U.S. And here in London is the heart of India also. Where are you now? I am passing through Geneva on my way to the Hills. I will be there a day or two.

If you be somewhere near, I will make it a point to come to see you. Did you hear Annie Besant? How did you like her? What about your plans of going to India next winter? What about the innocents (Mary and Harriet Hale and Isabelle and Harriet McKindley.) at home? I haven't had any news of them. My love to Father Pope, Mother Temple (Mrs. James Matthews, Mr. Hale's sister.) and yourself. Kindly answer as I will be only a few days here.

Ever yours with love and gratitude,

VIVEKANANDA

XCVI

A letter to the editor, which appeared in the July 11, 1896 issue of the Light

63, ST. GEORGE'S-ROAD, S.W.

SIR,

Allow me to put a few words in your estimable journal as comments on an article in your paper dated July 4th. I must thank you without reserve for the kind and friendly spirit manifested throughout the article towards me and the philosophy I preach; but, as there is a fear of misconstruction in one part of it — especially by my Spiritualistic friends — I want to clear my position. The truth of correspondence between the living and the dead is, I believe, in every religion, and nowhere more than in the Vedantic sects of India, where the fact of mutual help between the departed and the living has been made the basis of the law of inheritance. I would be very sorry if I be mistaken as antagonistic to any sect or form of religion, so far as they are sincere. Nor do I hold that any system can ever be judged by the frauds and failures that would naturally gather round every method under the present circumstances. But, all the same, I cannot but believe that every thoughtful person would agree with me when I affirm that people should be warned of their dangers, with love and sympathy. The lecture alluded to could but accidentally touch the subject of Spiritualism; but I take this opportunity of conveying my deep admiration for the Spiritualist community for the positive good they have done already, and are doing still: (1) the preaching of a universal sympathy; (2) the still greater work of helping the human race out of doctrines which inculcate fear and not love. Ever ready to co-operate with, and at the service of, all who are striving to bring the light of the spirit,

I remain yours sincerely,

VIVE KANANDA

XCVII

To Mrs. Ole Bull

63 ST. GEORGE'S ROAD

18th July '96

DEAR MRS. BULL,

I received your last note duly — and you already know my gratitude and love for you and that I perfectly agree with most of your ideas and work.

I did not understand, however, one point. You speak of Sturdy and myself being members. Members of what? I, as you well know, can not become a member of any society.

I am very glad to learn that you have been favourably impressed by Saradananda. There is one big mistake you are labouring under. What do you mean of [my] writing to my workers more confidentially and not to you? I seldom write to anyone — I have no time to write. I have no workers. Everyone is independent to work as one likes. I do not bother my head about these little things at all. I can give ideas — that is all; let people work them out any way they like, and Godspeed to all.

"He who works unattached to persons and giving up the fruits of work is a genuine worker" — Gitâ.

Yours Ever with love and gratitude,

VIVEKANANDA

XCVIII

To Sister Christine

[POSTMARKED: SAAS-FEE]

SWITZERLAND

5th August 1896

BLESSED AND BELOVED,

Surrounded on all sides by eternal snow peaks, sitting on the grass in a beautiful wood, my thoughts go to those I love — so I write.

I am in Switzerland — constantly on the move — getting a much needed rest. It is a miniature Himalayas, and has the same effect of raising the mind up to the Self and driving away all earthly feelings and ties. I am intensely enjoying it. I feel so, so uplifted. I cannot write, but I wish you will have the same for ever — when your feet do not want, as it were, to touch the material earth — when the soul finds itself floating, as it were, in an ocean of spirituality.

Prof. Max Müller has written in the *Nineteenth Century* an article on my Master. Read it if you can — August number.

I hope you are enjoying this beautiful summer and are perfectly rested after hard work.

My love to all. Blessings to all.

Yours ever with love and blessings,

VIVEKANANDA

P.S. A few Alpine flowers growing almost in the midst of eternal snow I send you, praying that you may attain spiritual hardihood amidst all snows and ice of this life.

XCIX

To Sister Christine

AIRLIE LODGE, RIDGEWAY GARDENS

WIMBLEDON, ENGLAND

October 6, 1896

DEAR CHRISTINA,

I am sure you got my letter from Switzerland.

I am now in London, back after having travelled through Germany and Holland.

How are things going with you? Had you a nice summer? How are you physically and spiritually? How is Mrs. Fhunkey [Funke] and all the other friends? Have you any news of Baby? Where is Kr [Kripananda] and what is he doing now?

I have another Sannyasin over here with me now, who will work here whilst I am away to India, where I go this winter.

I will write to you *in extenso* later; tonight it is so late and I am so weary.

With all love and blessings,

Yours,

VIVEKANANDA

C

To Sister Nivedita

14, GREYCOAT GARDENS

WESTMINSTER

October 29, 1896

DEAR MISS [MARGARET] NOBLE —

I will be at yours on Friday next, at 4 p.m.

I did not know of any arrangements made to meet anybody Friday last, hence my absence.

Yours,

VIVEKANANDA

CI

To Sister Nivedita

14, GREYCOAT GARDENS

WESTMINSTER, S.W.

5 December 1896

DEAR MISS NOBLE –

Many thanks for sending the kind present from Mr. Beatty. I have written to him acknowledging his beautiful gift.

As for you, my dear, noble, kind friend, I only would say this – we Indians lack in many things, but there is none on earth to beat us in gratefulness. I remain,

Ever yours gratefully,

VIVEKANANDA

CII

To Sister Christine

ON BOARD PRINZ REGENT LUITPOLD

3rd January 1897.

DEAR CHRISTINA,

By two p.m. today I reach Port Said. Asia once more. I have not heard from you [for] long. Hope everything is going on well with you. How are Mrs. Funke, Mrs. Phelps, and all other friends?

My love to all. Write when you feel like it.

VIVEKANANDA.

CIII

To the Madras Committee

[After Swami Vivekananda Colombo on Friday, January 15, 1897, the Madras Committee, which was planning a reception for the Swami, sent the following message: "Motherland rejoices to welcome you back". In reply, Swami Vivekananda sent a wire.]

[Postmarked: January 15, 1897]

MY LOVE AND GRATITUDE TO MY COUNTRYMEN.

CIV

To the Hindu Students of Trichinapally

[February 16, 1897]

GENTLEMEN,

I have received your address with great pleasure and sincerely thank you for the kind expressions contained therein.

I much regret, however, that time effectually prevents my paying even a short visit to Trichinopoly at present. In the autumn, however, I propose making a lecture tour throughout India, and you may rely upon it that I shall then not fail to include Trichinopoly in the programme.

Again thanking you, and with my blessings to all.

Sincerely yours,

VIVEKANANDA.

CV

To Sister Christine

DARJEELING,

[RETURN ADDRESS: ALAMBAZAR MATH, CALCUTTA]

16th March 1897.

DEAR CHRISTINA,

Many, many thanks for the photograph and the poem. I never saw anything half as beautiful. The work I had to do to reach Calcutta from Ceylon was so immense that I could not earlier acknowledge your precious gift. The work has broken me down completely, and I have got "diabetes", an incurable disease, which must carry me off — at least in a few years.

I am now writing to you from Darjeeling, the nearest hill station to Calcutta, with a climate as cool as London. It has revived me a bit. If I live, I will come to America next year or so.

How are things going on with you all? How are Mrs. Funkey [Funke] and Mrs. Phelps?

Are you laying by a few dollars whenever you can? That is very important.

I am in a hurry for the mail. You will be glad to know that the Indian people have, as it were, risen in a mass to honour me. I am the idol of the day. Mr. Goodwin is going to publish in book form all the addresses given to me and the speeches in reply. The demonstrations all over have been simply unique.

Yours with all love,

VIVEKANANDA.

CVI

To Mrs. Ole Bull

ALAMBAZAR MATH

CALCUTTA

[DARJEELING]

26th March 1897

DEAR MRS. BULL —

The demonstrations and national jubilations over me are over — at least I had to cut them short, as my health broke completely down. The result of this steady work in the West and the tremendous work of a month in India upon the Bengalee constitution is "diabetes". It is a hereditary foe and is destined to carry me off, at best, in a few years' time. Eating only meat and drinking no water seems to be the only way to prolong life — and, above all, perfect rest for the brain. I am giving my brain the needed rest in Darjeeling, from where I am writing you now.

I am so glad to hear about Saradananda's success. Give him my best love and do not allow him [to] do too *much work*. The Bengalee body is not the same as the American.

Mr. Chatterjy (Mohini) came to see me in Calcutta, and he was very friendly. I gave him your message. He is quite willing to work with me. Nothing more to write, only I am bent upon seeing my monastery started; and as soon as that is done, I come to America once more.

By the by, I will send to you a young lady from England — one Gertrude Orchard. She has been a governess, but she has talent in art etc., and I wished her to try her chance in America. I will give her a letter to you and Mrs. [Florence] Adams.

With my love to Mrs. Adams, Miss Thursby, Miss Farmer (the noble sister) and all the rest of our friends.

With eternal love and gratitude,

Yours affectionately,

VIVEKANANDA

CVII

(Translated from Bengali)

To Pandit Ram Ram Samjami

DARJEELING

[April] 1897

DEAR RAM RAM,

I received your first letter in Calcutta. I was busy there, and so it seems that I forgot to reply. You have deplored this in your letter, but that is not right. I do not forget anyone — especially those who have received grace from "Him".

While I was in England, I received your Avadhuta-Gitâ. It is beautifully printed. You mentioned *Karma-Yoga* — I do not have that book with me. It was printed in Madras. If there are any copies at the Math, I shall ask them to send one to you.

I have been very sick, so right now I am staying at Darjeeling. As soon as I feel better, I shall return to Calcutta. . . .

Please accept my special love. I pray for your welfare always.

Yours etc.,

VIVEKANANDA

CVIII

To Sister Nivedita

DARJEELING,

3rd April 1897.

DEAR MISS NOBLE,

I have just found a bit of important work for you to do on behalf of the downtrodden masses of India.

The gentleman I take the liberty of introducing to you is in England on behalf of the Tiyas, a plebeian caste in the native State of Malabar.

You will realize from this gentleman what an amount of tyranny there is over these poor people, simply because of their caste.

The Indian Government has refused to interfere on grounds of non-interference in the internal administration of a native State. The only hope of these people is the English Parliament. Do kindly everything in your power to help this matter [in] being brought before the British Public.

Ever yours in the truth,

VIVEKANANDA.

CIX

To Lala Badri Sah of Almora

DARJEELING

7th April '97.

DEAR LALAJEE,

Just received your kind invitation through telegram. Perhaps you have already heard that I have been attacked by "Diabetes", a fell disease.

That unsettled all our plans, and I had to run up to Darjeeling, it being very cool and very good for the disease.

I have felt much better since, and the doctors therefore do not want me to move about, as that brings about a relapse. If my present state of health continues for a month or two, I think I will be in a condition to come down to the plains and come to Almora to see you all. I am very sorry that I have caused you a good deal of trouble, but you see it could not be helped — the body was not under my control.

With all love to yourself and other friends in Almora.

Yours affectionately,

VIVEKANANDA

CX

To Lala Badri Sah

DEVALDHAR BAGICHA,

Thursday, [June 1897]

DEAR BADRI SAH,

I have been very sorry to learn that you are not well. It would please me very much if you would come down here for a few days, at any rate, with us; and I am sure it would do you good.

Yours with blessings,

VIVEKANANDA

CXI

To Mrs. Francis Leggett

ALMORA

20 June '97

DEAR MOTHER —

Herewith I take the liberty to introduce to you Miss Tremayne of London, a particular friend of mine going over to the States.

Any help given to her would greatly oblige.

Yours in the Lord,

VIVEKANANDA

CXII

To Mrs. Ole Bull

ALMORA

20 June '97

DEAR MRS. BULL —

Herewith I take the liberty of introducing Miss Tremayne of London.

I like nothing so much as being serviceable to young and energetic persons — and any help given to her in America will greatly oblige.

Yours in the Lord,

VIVEKANANDA

CXIII

To Mr. Sokanathan, Colombo

ALMORA

30th June 1897.

MY DEAR FRIEND,

The bearer of this note, Swami Shivananda, is [being] sent to Ceylon, as promised by me during my sojourn. He is quite fit for the work entrusted to his care, of course, with your kind help.

I hope you will introduce him to other Ceylon friends.

Yours ever in the Lord,

VIVEKANANDA

CXIV

(Translated from Bengali)

To Swami Shivananda

ALMORA,

The 9th July 1897

DEAR SHIVANANDA, (This address was written in English.)

I haven't received any word of your arrival yet. I heard that Alasinga has gone there with his relations by way of Jaipur. We stayed at the Binsar Dak Bungalow [rest-house] for two or three days, and then I left for Shyamdhura. At this, Miss [Henrietta] Müller got infuriated and left for Almora. Terribly upset, Miss Müller accused Shivananda of telling her first that I shall live with a friend as his guest and of renting later such a big house for the season at 80 rupees without consulting her. Very cross with everybody, she has been reproving one and all but has cooled down a little when I said I would pay half of the rent. . . .

Shashi himself [Swami Ramakrishnananda] should handle the entire amount of 100 rupees which the Raja of Ramnad is donating (every month); he should send a detailed account of the monthly income and expenditure to the Math — otherwise there won't be any check. Advise him to spend as little as necessary on Thakur's worship, for the money is [primarily] "for propagation of Truth". (The phrase "for propagation of Truth" was written in English.)

In case Gupta [Swami Sadananda] has lost his mental balance, ask him to come to Almora — but only when the boy selected for Shashi reaches there. I received a letter from R. A. [Rajam Aiyer?]. The money he sent has reached the Math. I have received two volumes of Ramanuja's commentary. Advise him to send me the third. Ask G. G. [Narasimhachari] to send me similar commentaries by Madhva and others, if he can.

A public meeting will have to be organized at Madras to present an address of welcome to the Raja [Ajit Singh] of Khetri and to Pratap Singh of Jodhpur for their boldness in visiting England as well as for representing their principalities in India in the Jubilee celebration. This has to be done on their return to India, but for that you have to endeavour from now on. Please go to Colombo and arrange a similar public meeting there.

Give my love to Kidi [Singaravelu Mudaliar] and Doctor [Nanjunda Rao]; ask Kidi why he hasn't written to me. What is wrong with him? Has he lost his devotion? Bear this in mind that you should not assume a teacher's place in the beginning. Do all your work with humility; otherwise everything will crumble to pieces. Please see that there is no opposition, criticism or obstacles to Shashi's work in Madras, for everybody should obey him — whoever may be in charge of a particular centre. If Shashi goes to Ceylon, he will have to obey your authority, etc. Make sure that every centre sends a weekly report to the Math. I have not seen a single one from Shashi yet. "O Rama! How hard it is to turn a donkey into a horse, even by beating!"

Above all "obedience" and "esprit de corps". The work cannot succeed unless there is perfect obedience to the authority of the Order and sacrifice of individual views for the sake of the Order. *Trinair gunatvam âpannair badhyante mattadantinah* — "Blades of grass woven into a rope can restrain even mad elephants".

With love to Sashi and Gupta,

VIVEKANANDA

CXV

To Sister Christine

KHETRI,

13th December 1897.

MY DEAR CHRISTINA,

How funny all these dreams and evil prognostications of yours! You don't want to send me evil influences by thinking that way of me! I will be only too glad to lose 50 lbs. of my weight. A little rest puffs me up, and I am the same bloated monk as ever.

I am all right except [for] a bad cold the last few days, owing to exposure and travel in the desert. I thank you for the letter though. I am pleased with it enormously, as it shows the mind.

Give Mrs. Funkey [Funke], Baby [Stella Campbell], and all the rest my love, and, as you know, yourself —

Yours ever in the Lord,

VIVEKANANDA.

PS — I will write a better note when this cold has left.

CXVI

To Sister Christine

JODHPUR, RAJPUTANA,

4th January 1898.

Love and greetings etc. to thee, dear Christina, and a happy New Year. May it find you younger in heart, stronger in body, and purer in spirit.

I am still travelling in season and out of season. Lecturing some, working a good deal.

Have you seen Mr. [Edward T.] Sturdy of England, who, I learn, has been to Detroit? Did you like him?

I am quite well and strong. Hope to meet you this blessed year again in America.

I am going to Calcutta in a few days, where I intend to be the rest of this cold weather. Next summer, I start for England or America most probably.

Yours ever in the Lord,

VIVEKANANDA.

CXVII

To Sister Nivedita

CALCUTTA

30th January 1898

MY DEAR MISS NOBLE,

This is to introduce Prof. M. Gupta, who has been already introduced to you on board the boat that brought you over to shore.

He has very kindly consented to devote an hour or more every day to teach you Bengali. I need not state that he is a genuine, good and great soul.

Ever yours in the Lord,

VIVEKANANDA

P.S. I am afraid you felt badly today.

CXVIII

To Sister Christine

THE MATH, BELOOR, HOWRAH DIST.,

BENGAL, INDIA,

11th March 1898.

MY DEAR CHRISTINA,

I simply wonder what has become of you. It is an age [that] I did not hear from you, and I expected so much after Sturdy's visit to Detroit. How did you like the man? What about Baby and the Devendorfs? How is Mrs. Funkey [Funke]? What are you going to do this summer? Take rest, dear Christina; I am sure you require it badly.

Mrs. Bull of Boston and Miss MacLeod of New York are now in India. We have changed our Math from the old, nasty house to a house on the banks of the Ganges. This is much more healthy and beautiful. We have also got a good piece of land very near on the same side where Mrs. Bull and Miss MacLeod are putting up now. It is wonderful how they accommodate themselves to our Indian life of privation and hardship! My, these Yanks can do anything! After the luxuries of Boston and New York, to be quite content and happy in this wretched little house!! We intend to travel a bit together in Kashmir, and *then* I come to America with them and am sure to get a hearty welcome from my friends. What do you think? Is it welcome news to you? Of course, I cannot undergo the same amount of work as before; that, dear Christina, I am sorry, I will no more be able to do. I will do a little work and [take] a good deal of rest. No more getting crowds and making noise, but quiet, silent, personal work will be all I intend to do.

This time I will quietly come and quietly go away, seeing only my old friends, and no noise.

Write soon, as I am so anxious.

Ever yours in the Lord,

VIVEKANANDA.

"There are two sorts of persons — one sort has the heart of water, the other of stone. The one easily takes an impression, and as easily throws it off; the other seldom takes an impression, but once it takes, it is there for ever. Nay, the more they struggle to cast it off, the more it cuts deep into the stone soul." — R. K. [Ramakrishna] Paramahamsa

CXIX

To Sister Nivedita

MATH, BELUR.

HOWRAH, BENGAL.

16th March 1898.

MY DEAR MARGARET,

It is needless to let you know, you have fulfilled all my expectations in your last lecture.

It appears to me that the platform is the great field where you will be of great help to me, apart from your educational plans. I am glad to learn that Miss [Henrietta] Müller is going to have a place on the river. Are you also going to Darjeeling? So you will all the better work after a trip up there! Next season I am planning a series of lectures for you all over India.

Ever yours with all love and blessings,

[Stamp with Swamiji's portrait]

THE CALCUTTA BOY.

CXX

To Mrs. Ole Bull

DARJEELING

the 4th April '98

MY DEAR DHIRA MATA —

I am afraid you are getting roasted down there in the heat of Calcutta. Here it is nice and cool and rather chill when it rains, which it does almost every day. Yesterday the view of the snows was simply superb, and it is the most picturesque city in the world; there is such a mass of colour everywhere, especially in the dress of the Lepchas and Bhutias and the Paharees. Had it not been for the awful, corrugated iron roofs everywhere, it would have been twenty times more picturesque.

My health was not bad in Calcutta; here it is the same — only, the sugar has entirely disappeared, the specific gravity being only 13. I slept very well last night too; but the morning ride up, or climb, of a few miles is proving too much for my adipose tissues. The flannel clothes only made me worse, so I have given them up and have gone to my summer dress and am all right.

I have sent you Sturdy's letter already — poor fellow — I do not know what to do for him. He is really "living in a desert of his own making" — you see, one thing is not good for every one. Marriage has indeed proved a hell for Sturdy. And he can not come, although "he is skirting the coast of India". Lord help the poor boy. May He cut all his bonds and make him free soon. Aye, it is good that he is feeling the bondage — and not "hugging and kissing its spokes of agony".

I gave a little lecture to the Hindus here yesterday, and I told them all their defects purposely and with their permission. I hope it will make them howl.

Miss Müller has taken a bungalow here and she is coming on Wednesday. I do not know whether Miss Noble is coming with her. She [Miss Noble] had better be your guest in Kashmir as according to our plan.

Have you got that place yet or changed [places]? I am going to Kashmir anyway, as I have promised.

I will be here only a few days and then I come to Calcutta, to be there only a week — and [then] I start for the N.W. Of course this is not the time to see anything in the N.W.P.; (North-West Provinces, now Uttar Pradesh.) everything is burning there. Yet that heat is much healthier than that of Bengal.

Ever yours in the Lord,

VIVEKANANDA

CXXI

To Munshi Jagmohanlal

BALLEN VILLE

DARJEELING

15 April 1898

MY DEAR JAGMOHAN,

If you can find out all the letters that I addressed to H.H. on my way to — and stay in — Japan, Europe and America, please do send them carefully packed, under registered cover, to my address in the Math, as early as possible.

With blessing to you,

I remain,

Yours truly,

VIVEKANANDA

CXXII

To Miss Josephine MacLeod

DARJEELING

19th April '98

MY DEAR MISS MACLEOD,

Miss Müller is very glad to learn that you intend inviting Miss Noble to join our party to Kashmir.

It has her hearty approval. On her way back, Miss Müller will start something for her in Calcutta. She need not come to Darjeeling at all.

Hope you are enjoying the baking quite a bit. I start this week most probably.

Ever yours in the Lord,

VIVEKANANDA

CXXIII

To the Officer in Charge of Telegrams, Srinagar

April 19, 1898.

SIR,

Please allow Miss M'cLeod [MacLeod] or her agent to receive any telegrams that you have received for me and receipt the same.

Yours truly,

VIVEKANANDA

CXXIV

To Miss Josephine MacLeod or Mrs. Ole Bull

SESHNAG

CHANDANBARI, KASHMIR

[EN ROUTE FROM SRINAGAR TO AMARNATH]

[End of July 1898]

I send back the old Dandi (A simple palanquin.) as it is difficult to carry it through. I have got another like Margaret's. Please send it back to the Tahsildar of Vernag, Khand Chand, Esq., whom you already know. We are all right. Margot has discovered some new flowers and is happy. There is not much ice so the road is good.

Yours affectionately,

VIVEKANANDA

P.S. Keep this Dandi till I come and pay the coolies (2) 4 Rs., 2 annas each.

Coolie — Tara

[Accounts List]

[Illegible word] 20

Dandi	26		
Coolies 16	2 hrs.	=8 Rs.	— as.
Coolies 4	2½ hrs. at 4 as. per hr.	=2	— 8
Dandi 26	3½ hrs. at 6 as. per hr.	34	— 2
4 extra	1 hr. at 4 as. per hr.	=1	— 0
2 ponies	2½ hrs. at 12 as. per hr.	=3	— 12
1 pony 1 hr.	at 12 as. per hr.	=0	— 12

		50	– 2
2 Dandis	3″ hrs.	[Illegible words]	
		52	– 0
	[Illegible words]	8	– [0]
		60	– [0]

Bed chairs 4

Luggage 25

Dandi 26

55

55 *all inclusive*

Two horses—— 1st stage——12 miles

Batacooti——

Phahalgaon [Pahalgam] — next stage

CXXV

To Mr. J. J. Goodwin's mother

[On receiving news of the untimely death of Josiah J. Goodwin, Swami Vivekananda sent the following paragraph along with the poem "Requiescat in Pace" (This poem has been previously published in Complete Works, IV.) to the newspapers as well as to Goodwin's mother.]

ALMORA

June 1898

With infinite sorrow I learn the sad news of Mr. Goodwin's departure from this life, the more so as it was terribly sudden and therefore prevented all possibilities of my being at his side at the time of death. The debt of gratitude I owe him can never be repaid, and those who think they have been helped by any thought of mine ought to know that almost every word of it was published through the untiring and most unselfish exertions of Mr. Goodwin. In him I have lost a friend true as steel, a disciple of never — failing devotion, a worker who knew not what tiring was, and the world is less rich by one of those few who are born, as it were, to live only for others.

[UNSIGNED]

CXXVI

To Maharaja Ajit Singh, the Raja of Khetri

SRINAGAR

10 August 1898

YOUR HIGHNESS—

I have long not heard any news of you. How are things going on with you both bodily and mentally?

I have been to see Shri Amarnathji. It was a very enjoyable trip and the Darshana was glorious.

I will be here about a month more, then I return to the plains. Kindly ask Jagmohan to write to the Dewan Saheb of Kishangarh to get for me the copies of Nimbârka Bhâshya which he promised.

With all love,

Yours,

VIVEKANANDA

CXXVII

To Sister Christine

THE MATH, BELOOR, HOWRAH DIST.,

25th October, 1898.

MY DEAR CHRISTINA,

How are you? I am very anxious about your health. I have long not had any letter from you.

My health again failed badly. I had, therefore, to leave Kashmir in haste and come to Calcutta. The doctors say I ought not go tramping again this winter. That is such a disappointment, you know. However, I am coming to the U. S. this summer. Mrs. Bull and Miss MacLeod enjoyed this year's trip to Kashmir immensely, and now they are having a glimpse of the old monuments and buildings of Delhi, Agra, Jeypore [Jaipur], etc.

Do write a nice, long letter if you have time, and do not work yourself to death. Duty is duty, no doubt; but we have our duties, not only to our mother etc., but to others also. Sometimes one duty asks for physical sacrifice, whilst the other insists on great care for our health. Of course, we follow the stronger motive, and [I] do not know which will prove stronger in your case. Anyhow, take great care of your body, now that your sisters have come to your help.

How do you manage the family? — the expenses etc? Write me all you like to write. Give me a long chat, will you? Do!

I am getting better every day — and then the long months before I can start for the U.S. Never mind, "Mother" knows what is best for us. She will show the way. I am now in Bhakti. As I am growing old, Bhakti is taking the place of Jnâna. Did you get the new *Awakened India*? How do you like it?

Ever yours in the Lord,

VIVEKANANDA

CXXVIII

Maharaja Ajit Singh, the Raja of Khetri

MATH BELUR

22 November 1898

YOUR HIGHNESS —

Many thanks for your kind note and the Nimbarka Bhashya — reached through Jaga Mohan Lalji.

I approach your Highness today on a most important business of mine, knowing well that I have not the least shame in opening my mind to you, and that I consider you as my *only friend* in this life. If the following appeals to you, good; if not, pardon my foolishness as a friend should.

As you know already, I have been ailing since my return. In Calcutta your Highness assured me of your friendship and help for me personally and [advised me] not to be worried about this incurable malady. This disease has been caused by nervous excitement; and no amount of change can do me good, unless the worry and anxiety and excitement are taken off me.

After trying these two years a different climate, I am getting worse every day and now almost at death's door. I appeal to your Highness's work, generosity and friendship. I have one great sin rankling always in my breast, and that is [in order] to do a service to the world, I have sadly neglected my mother. Again, since my second brother has gone away, she has become awfully worn-out with grief. Now my last desire is to make Sevâ [give service] and serve my mother, for some years at least. I want to live with my mother and get my younger brother married to prevent extinction of the family. This will certainly smoothen my last days as well as those of my mother. She lives now in a hovel. I want to build a little, decent home for her and make some provision for the youngest, as there is very little hope of his being a good earning man. Is it too much for a royal descendent of Ramchandra to do for one he loves and calls his friend? I do not know whom else to appeal to. The money I got from Europe was for the "work", and every penny almost has been given over to that work. Nor can I beg of others for help for my own self. About my own family affairs — I have exposed myself to your Highness, and none else shall know of it. I am tired, heartsick and dying. Do, I pray, this last great work of kindness to me, befitting your great and generous nature and [as] a crest to the numerous kindnesses you have shown me. And as your Highness will make my last days smooth and easy, may He whom I have tried to serve all my life ever shower His choicest blessings on you and yours.

Ever yours in the Lord,

VIVEKANANDA

P.S. This is strictly private. Will you please drop a wire to me whether you will do it or not?

Ever yours,

VIVEKANANDA

CXXIX

To Maharaja Ajit Singh, the Raja of Khetri

MATH BELOOR

HOWRAH DISTRICT

1 December 1898

YOUR HIGHNESS –

Your telegram has pleased me beyond description, and it is worthy of your noble self. I herewith give you the details of what I want.

The lowest possible estimate of building a little home in Calcutta is at least ten thousand rupees. With that it is barely possible to buy or build a house in some out-of-the-way quarter of the town – a little house fit for four or five persons to live in.

As for the expenses of living, the 100 Rs. a month your generosity is supplying my mother is enough for her. If another 100 Rs. a month be added to it for my lifetime for my expenses – which unfortunately this illness has increased, and which, I hope, will not be for long a source of trouble to you, as I expect only to live a few years at best – I will be perfectly happy. One thing more will I beg of you – if possible, the 100 Rs. a month for my mother be made permanent, so that even after my death it may regularly reach her. Or even if your Highness ever gets reasons to stop your love and kindness for me, my poor old mother may be provided [for], remembering the love you once had for a poor Sâdhu.

This is all. Do this little work amongst the many other noble deeds you have done, knowing well whatever else can be proved or not, the power of Karma is self-evident to all. The blessings of this good Karma shall always follow you and yours. As for me, what shall I say – whatever I am in the world has been almost all through your help. You made it possible for me to get rid of a terrible anxiety and face the world and do some work. It may be that you are destined by the Lord to be the instrument again of helping yet grander work, by taking this load off my mind once more.

But whether you do this or not, "once loved is always loved". Let all my love and blessings and prayers follow you and yours, day and night, for what I owe you already; and may the Mother, whose play is this universe and in whose hands we are mere instruments, always protect you from all evil.

Ever yours in the Lord,

VIVEKANANDA

CXXX

To Sister Nivedita

3 p.m. Sunday.

[Early 1899]

MY DEAR MARGOT,

I am sorry I cannot come to see Dr. Mahoney — I am ill. I have not yet broken my fast.

Have you stopped teaching my little cousin?

Yours with love,

VIVEKANANDA

CXXXI

To Sister Nivedita

[Early 1899?]

MY DEAR NIVEDITA,

The address of my cousin is 127 Manicktala Street. The husband's name is Durga Prasanna Bose. The wife's name is most probably not known to the people you will meet in the male department. Therefore it is the custom to ask for the wife of so-and-so.

Manicktala Street is that which runs east and west, south of the tank garden.

Yours with love,

VIVEKANANDA

CXXXII

To Sister Christine

THE MATH, BELUR,
DIST. HOWRAH, BENGAL, INDIA,
26th January 1899.

MY DEAR CHRISTINA,

Excuse this long delay in replying to your very beautiful note. The fact is, I was once more in the vale of death. The old diabetes has now disappeared. In its place has come what some doctors call asthma, others dyspepsia, owing to nervous prostration. However, it is a most worrying disease, giving one the sensation of suffocation — sometimes for days. I am best only in Calcutta; so I am here for rest and quiet and low diet. If I get well by March, I am going to start for Europe. Mrs. Bull and others are gone; sorry I could not accompany them owing to this disease.

I have carefully weighed your plans for coming over. I will be ever so glad to see you, you know it well; but, my dear, the Indian summer will not suit you, and if you start now it will be midsummer when you reach India. Then, you must not hope of making any living here. It is impossible for me to make a living most times in my own country. Then all the surroundings are so, so wretched and different from what you see around you, e.g. you will find me going about in loin-cloth — will that shock you? Three-fourths of the population only wearing a strip of white cloth about their loins — can you bear that?

I must stop here; I am so weak. If I do not get well by March, I will write you to come, for I wish it ever so much to see you once before I pass away.

Do not be the least anxious, dear. Things must be as "Mother" wishes. Ours is only to obey and work.

Ever yours in the Lord,

VIVEKANANDA.

PS. Mrs. Bull will reach Cambridge, Mass., soon. You may write to her there on the particulars.

Yours,

PPS. I have again lost your address. Please give the correct one in your next.

CXXXIII

To Swami Brahmananda

THE MATH, BELUR

Friday [March (?) 1899]

MY DEAR RAJA,

Please pay 100 Rs. to Sister Nivedita immediately for plague work and credit it to a separate plague account.

Yours affectionately,

VIVEKANANDA

CXXXIV

To Swami Swarupananda, editor of
Prabuddha Bharata, Mayavati

[March 1899]

MY DEAR S[WARUPANANDA],

I have no objection whether Mrs. Sevier's name goes on top or mine or anybody else's; the prospectus ought to go in the name of the Seviers, mustering my name also if necessary. I send you a few lines for your consideration in the prospectus. The rest are all right.

I will soon send the draft deed.

CXXXV

To Sister Nivedita

THE MATH, BELUR,

March 2nd, 1899

MY DEAR MARGOT,

Will you look into your trunks for a Sanskrit book of mine, which was, you know, in your keeping in Kashmir. I do not find it in our library here.

I have been thinking of your friend Miss [Sarala] Ghosal's coming to see the Math on Sunday. The difficulty is here. The ebb tide will be on till 5 p.m. In that case our big boat can go down easily to bring the party up; and going back, if the party starts long before 5 p.m., say 4 p.m., will be all right. To come up will take at least two hours from Baghbazar. If the party starts from Baghbazar — say at 12 a.m. — and reaches the Math at 2 p.m. for lunch and then starts back by 4 p.m., it will be nice.

If you cannot start as early as that, I will advise you to send the carriage to wait at Baranagore on the other side so that our boat can ferry the party over any time they like. The boat journey in that case will only be on coming.

With all love and blessings,

VIVEKANANDA

CXXXVI

To Ishwar Chandra Ghosh

MATH, BELUR

HOWRAH DIST.

6th March '99

MY DEAR SIR,

Many thanks for your kind invitation. I am so sorry that so many days' delay should occur in reply to your note.

I was very ill at the time, and the gentleman on whom the duty fell of replying could not do it, it seems. I got notice of it just now.

I am not yet sufficiently recovered to take advantage of your kindness. This winter I had made it a point of visiting your part of the country. But my Karma will have otherwise. I will have to wait to give myself the pleasure of visiting the seat of civilisation of ancient Bengal.

With my thanks again for all your kindness, I remain,

Yours in the Lord,

VIVEKANANDA

CXXXVII

To Sister Nivedita

THE MATH, BELUR,

April 25th, 1899

MY DEAR MARGOT,

I could not come today. I am so, so sorry. The body would not allow — neither can I come to the Boses'. I have written to them.

I have an engagement tomorrow.

Possibly I may see you in the evening.

With all love and blessings,

VIVEKANANDA

CXXXVIII

To Sister Christine

THE MATH, BELUR,

DIST. HOWRAH, BENGAL, INDIA,

10th May 1899.

MY DEAR CHRISTINA,

I am getting better again. In my mind the whole of my complaint is bad assimilation of food and nervous exhaustion. The first, I am taking care of; the second will completely pass off when I meet you again. The great joy of meeting old, old friends, you know! Cheer up! There is no cause for anxiety. Do not believe a single desponding line I write now, because I am at times not myself. I get so nervous.

I start this summer for Europe anyway, as you say in America. With all love and blessings,

Yours ever in the Lord,

VIVEKANANDA.

CXXXIX

To Miss Josephine MacLeod

[When Swami Vivekananda sailed from Calcutta, he dispatched the following cablegram.]

[CALCUTTA,

June 21, 1899]

STARTED. WIRE STURDY.

CXL

To Sister Christine

SUEZ,

14th July 1899.

MY DEAR CHRISTINA,

You see this time I am really out, and hope to reach London in two weeks. I am sure to come to America this year and earnestly hope will have the opportunity of seeing you. I am so materialistic yet, you know! Want to see my friends in the gross body.

I had a beautiful letter from Baby [Stella Campbell] before I left. I am soon going to pen a reply to your care, as directed. I could not write her earlier.

I was so, so bad in health in India. My heart went wrong all the way — what with mountain climbing, bathing in glacier water and nervous prostration! I used to get terrible fits [of asthma] — the last lasting about seven days and nights. All the time I was suffocating and had to stand up.

This trip has almost made a new man of me. I feel much better and, if this continues, hope to be quite strong before I reach America. How are you? What are you doing? Write everything about yourself, c/o E. T. Sturdy Esq., 25 Holland Villas Road, London, W.

With everlasting love and blessings,

Ever yours in the Lord,

VIVEKANANDA.

CXLI

To Sister Christine

MARSEILLES,

23rd July 1899.

MY DEAR CHRISTINA,

Your very, very welcome wire just came. By next Sunday we arrive in London, Albert Dock. We are a party of four: myself, another Sannyasin, a Calcutta boy going to study in America, and Miss [Margaret] Noble. Miss Noble is a young lady from Wimbledon, near London, who has been working in India on the education of girls.

Our stay in England will not be long, I am afraid, as this is neither the season nor am I in fit condition to work much. Anyhow, we will be in London a few weeks — at least myself — then go to the U.S. We will talk over all this and infinite things besides when we meet. I do not think even English summer days are long enough for all the chatter I will assail you with.

We go to Wimbledon for a day or two, and then I come back to London and find lodgings for myself and make plans.

Come to the Dock if that is possible and discreet. Yes, it is discreet, as there is a lady in the party and others will come to meet her. Only, Christina, don't if you feel the least tired or unwell. I hope you are enjoying London immensely.

The Orientals do not like any effusion of feeling. They are trained to hide all expression.

Is Mrs. Funkey [Mary Caroline Funke] with you? If so, give her my best love.

I am much, much better just now. I am really quite another man this time. I was nearly dead in Calcutta when I started, but this voyage has improved me immensely.

Hoping soon to see you,

Ever yours in the Lord,

VIVEKANANDA.

CXLII

To Sister Christine

TELEGRAM

TO:

CHRISTINA GRINNSTIDEL [GREENSTIDEL]

23 CROWHURST RD., ANGELL RD.

BRIATON, LDN.

30 July 1899

GOLCONDA DUE DOCKS 6 AM MONDAY. (*Vide* Swami Vivekananda's letter dated July 23, 1899.)

CXLIII

To Mrs. Ole Bull

THE LYMES, WOODSIDE

WIMBLEDON, ENGLAND

6 August 1899

MY DEAR MOTHER,

Your letter directed to Sturdy at hand. I am very thankful for your kind words. As for me, I don't know what I am to do next or anything to do at all. On board the steamer I was all right, but since landing [I am] feeling quite bad again. As to mental worry, there has been enough of late. The aunt whom you saw had a deep-laid plan to cheat me, and she and her people contrived to sell me a house for 6,000 Rs., or £400, and I bought [it] for my mother in good faith. Then they would not give me possession, hoping that I would not go to court for the shame of taking forcible possession as a Sannyasin.

I do not think *I have spent even one rupee from what you and others gave me for the work*. Cap. Sevier gave me 8,000 Rs. with the express desire of helping my mother. This money, it seems, has [also] gone to the dogs. Beyond this, nothing has been spent on my family or even on *my own personal* expenses — my food etc. being paid for by the Khetri Raja, and more than half of that went to the Math every month. Only, if Brahmananda spends some in the lawsuit [against the aunt], as I must not be robbed that way — if he does, I will make it good anyway, if I live to do it.

The money which I got in Europe and America by *lecturing* alone, I spent just as I like; but every cent I got for the work has been accounted for and is in the Math, and the whole thing ought to be clear as daylight if Brahmananda never cheated me. I don't believe he will ever cheat me. I got a letter at Aden from Saradananda that they were preparing an account. I have not received any yet.

I have no plans yet, nor care to make any. Neither do I wish to work. Let the Mother find other workers. I have my burden enough already.

Ever your devoted son,

VIVEKANANDA

CXLIV

To Miss Isabelle McKindley

RIDGELY MANOR

STONE RIDGE, N.Y.

31st August '99

MY DEAR ISABEL —

Many thanks for your kind note. I will be so, so glad to see you. Miss M'cLeod [MacLeod] is going to write you to stop a day and a night here on your way to the West.

My love to the holy family in Chicago, and hope surely to be able to come West and have great fun.

So you are in Greenacre at last. Is this the first year you have been there? How do you like the place? [You have] seen Miss Farmer, of course. Kindly convey her my kindest regards and to all the rest of my friends there.

Ever yours affectionately,

VIVEKANANDA

CXLV

To Sister Christine

RIDGELY MANOR,

20th September 1899.

DEAR CHRISTINA,

I am much better, thank you. Hitherto, excepting three days, there has not been any wet weather to speak of here. Miss [Margaret] Noble came yesterday, and we are having a jolly good time. I am very, very sorry to say I am growing fat again. That is bad. I will eat less and grow thin once more.

You are again at work — so do I find — only with a little variation of the old occupation. Better rest than mere idling. Do you like my new poem? (Vide Complete Works, IV for the text of the poem "Peace" enclosed in this letter.) Miss Noble thinks it is nice. But that is her way with everything I do. So you also say. I will now send my writings to missionary papers to get a fierce criticism.

With all love to you and Mrs. Funkey [Funke],

Ever yours affectionately,

VIVEKANANDA.

CXLVI

To Mrs. G. W. Hale

RIDGELY MANOR

5 October 1899

MY DEAR MOTHER CHURCH,

Many, many thanks for your kind words.

I am so glad you are working on as ever. I am glad because the wave of optimism has not caught you yet. It is all very well to say everything is right, but that is apt to degenerate into a sort of *laissez-faire*. I believe with you that the world is evil – made more hideous with a few dashes of good.

All our works have only this value, that they awaken some to the reality of this horror – and [those] flee for refuge to some place beyond, which is called God, or Christ, or Brahma, or Buddha, etc. Names do not make much difference.

Again, we must always remember ours is only to work – we never attain results. How can we? Good can never be done without doing evil. We cannot breathe a breath without killing thousands of poor little animals. National prosperity is another name for death and degradation to millions of other races. So is individual prosperity the beggaring of many. The world is evil – and will ever remain so. It is its nature, and cannot be changed – "Which one of you by taking thought . . ." etc. (Matthew 6.27.)

Such is truth. The wisdom is therefore in renunciation, that is, to make the Lord our all in all. Be a true Christian, Mother – like Christ, renounce everything and let the heart and soul and body belong to Him and Him alone. All this nonsense which people have built round Christ's name is not His teaching. He taught to renounce. He never says the earth is an enjoyable place. And your time has come to get rid of all vanities – even the love of children and husband – and think of the Lord and Him alone.

Ever your Son,

VIVEKANANDA

CXLVII

To Mrs. G. W. Hale

[RIDGELY MANOR], NEW YORK, N.Y.

23 October 1899

MY DEAR MOTHER,

I was taking a few days' complete rest and so am late in replying to your very kind note. Accept my congratulations on the anniversary of your marriage. I pray many, many such returns may come to you.

I am sure my previous letter was coloured by the state of my body, as indeed is the whole of existence to us. Yet, Mother, there is more pain than pleasure in life. If not, why do I remember you and your children almost every day of my life, and not many others? Happiness is liked so much because it is so rare, is it not? Fifty percent of our life is mere lethargy, ennui; of the rest, forty percent is pain, only ten happiness — and this for the exceptionally fortunate. We are oft-times mixing up this state of ennui with pleasure. It is rather a negative state, whilst both pleasure and pain are nearer positive, though not positive.

Pleasure and pain are both *feeling*, not *willing*. They are only processes which convey to the mind excitements or motives of action. The real positive action is the willing, or impulse to work, of the mind — begun when the sensation has been taken in (pleasure and pain); thus the real is neither pleasure nor pain. It has no connection with either. Quite different from either. The barking of the dog awakens his master to guard against a thief or receive his dearest friend. It does not follow, therefore, that the dog and his master are of the same nature or have any degree of kinship. The feelings of pleasure or pain similarly awaken the soul to activity, without any kinship at all.

The soul is beyond pain, beyond pleasure, sufficient in its own nature. And no hell can punish it, nor any heaven can bless it. So far philosophy.

I am coming soon to Chicago, and hope to say "Lord bless you" to you and your children. All love as usual to my Christian relatives, scientific or quacks.

VIVEKANANDA

CXLVIII

To Sister Christine

C/O F. H. LEGGETT, ESQ.,

RIDGELY MANOR,

STONE RIDGE, ULSTER CO., N.Y.

25th October 1899.

DEAR CHRISTINA,

What is the matter with you? Write me a line to tell me how you are and what you are doing now.

I am tired of this place, and will come down to New York for a few days soon. I start thence for Chicago and, if you like, will stop at Detroit on my way to How-do-you-do. I am much better, indeed quite a different man, though not completely cured — for that, time is necessary.

Yours,

VIVEKANANDA.

CXLIX

To Sister Christine

RIDGELY MANOR,

30th October 1899.

MY DEAR CHRISTINA,

Did you not get my last letter? I am very anxious to know how you are. Write a line to tell me you are in very good health.

I am afraid the previous one was misdirected, so I send this c/o Mrs. Funkey [Funke].

Do write soon. I am thinking of Battle Creek food. Baby insists on that. Do you think it will do me any good? Write soon.

Ever yours in the Lord,

VIVEKANANDA.

PS — Where is this Battle Creek? Is it near Detroit? I am seriously thinking of giving it a trial. I am not bad, but unfit for any exertion, even for a walk. This sort of life is no good to live. I [will] try Battle Creek, and if that fails, get out quick.

Write me about Battle Creek.

CL

To Sister Christine

RIDGELY MANOR,

4th November 1899.

MY DEAR CHRISTINA,

The letter was all right in reaching. It was only my nervousness. I am sure you will understand and excuse this. I eagerly expect t o see you in Cambridge. I am going to New York next week. Thence I go for a few days to Washington and then to Cambridge. Do come. And mind you, I must learn German. I am determined to be a French and German scholar. French, I think, I can manage with the help of a dictionary. If I can do that much German in a month, I will be so glad.

It naturally takes time for a letter to reach from here. We have one delivery and one posting a day.

With all love,

Ever yours in the Lord,

VIVEKANANDA.

My eternal love and blessings to Mrs. Funkey [Funke].

CLI

To Sister Christine

21 WEST 34TH STREET,

NEW YORK,

10th November 1899.

MY DEAR CHRISTINA,

I received your letter just now. I am now in New York. Dr. [Egbert] Guernsey analysed my urine yesterday, and there was no sugar or albumen in it. So my kidneys are all right, at least at present. The heart is only nervous, requires calming! — some cheerful company and good, loving friends and quiet. The only difficulty is the *dyspepsia*, and that is the evil. For instance, I am all right in the morning and can walk miles, but in the evening it is impossible to walk after a meal — the gas — that depends entirely up on food, does it not? I ought to try the Battle Creek food. If I come to Detroit, there will be quiet and Battle Creek food for me.

But if you come to Cambridge with all the instructions of the Battle Creek food, I will have it prepared there; or, between you and me, we will cook it. I am a good hand at that. You don't know a thing about cooking. Well, you may help in cleaning the plates etc. I always get money when I need it badly. "Mother" always sees to that. So, no danger on that head. I am not in the least danger of life, the Doctors agree — only if this dyspepsia goes away. And that is "food", "food", "food", and no worry. Oh, what a worry I have had! Say we go somewhere else and make a little party and keep house ourselves. In Cambridge, Mrs. Bull has a quiet separate place — her studio house. You can have rooms there. I wish you to know Mrs. Bull. She is a saint, a real saint, if ever there was one. Wait for my next letter. I will write today again, or tomorrow after seeing Mrs. Bull.

Ever yours in the Lord,

VIVEKANANDA.

CLII

To Sister Christine

C/O DR. E. GUERNSEY,

180 WEST 59TH STREET,

NEW YORK,

12th November 1899.

CHRISTINA —

Mrs. Bull has gone to Boston without seeing me. I am with the Guernseys. All today laid up with colds.

Oh, these nasty colds. The doctor here declares my case as entirely one of nervous exhaustion. Even the dyspepsia is entirely nervous.

I will be a few days yet here, and then I don't know where I go. I have a great mind to try health food. As for you, write unreservedly where you [would] like me to be. If you think it best for me to come to Detroit, write or wire on receipt of this. I will come immediately. Only difficulty is now the dyspepsia.

With love to Mrs. Funkey [Funke],

Ever yours with blessings,

VIVEKANANDA.

P.S. If Cambridge is best, say that immediately.

CLIII

To Mrs. Ole Bull

180 W. 59,

C/O E. GUERNSEY, M.D.,

12 November 1899

DEAR MRS. BULL —

I am laid up with a bad cold. The clothes are not ready — they will be next week. I don't know what my next step will be. Dr. Guernsey is very kind. Several Doctors have examined me and none could detect any organic disease.

Even the kidney complications for the present have disappeared.

Well, the whole thing is then dyspepsia. I want ever so much to try Battle Creek food. There is a restaurant which cooks only Battle Creek food. Do you think it should be best for me to try it just now? If so, I go to Detroit. In that case, send me my terracotta, thick cashmere coat.

Ever yours in the Lord,

VIVEKANANDA

Had three treatments already from Helmer. Going to take some next week. None can do anything for this "wind". That is why dieting should be tried at any cost.

CLIV

To Sister Christine

21 WEST 34TH STREET,

NEW YORK,

21st November 1899.

MY DEAR CHRISTINA,

Circumstances have so fallen that I have to start for California tomorrow. It is for my physical benefit too; as the doctor says, I had better be off where the severe winter of the North cannot reach.

Well, thus my plans are made and marred. Anyway — come over to Cambridge when you feel like it. Mrs. Bull will only be too happy to do anything for you she can.

I hope to stop in Detroit on my way back. The Lord's will — as we say.

Ever yours in the Lord,

VIVEKANANDA.

CLV

To Mrs. Ole Bull

CHICAGO

30 November 1899

MY DEAR DHIRA MATA —

I am going to leave this place tonight. They have given me a new trunk — a big one. The Maspero book is with me, only the second volume. The first volume must be in Boston. Kindly send it c/o Joe [Miss Josephine MacLeod].

They have been very kind. Madame [Emma] Calvé, came to see me day before yesterday. She is a great woman.

I have nothing to write here except that Margo [Sister Nivedita] is doing very well, except some people were complaining last night that she frightened them with her assertion that Swami can not make mistakes!!!

Hope things are going on with you very well. This is in haste. I write in length from California.

Ever your son,

VIVEKANANDA

My love to Mrs. [Olea] Vaughn. (Mrs. Ole Bull's daughter.)

CLVI

To Mrs. G. W. Hale

THE CALIFORNIA LIMITED

SANTA FE ROUTE

1 December 1899

MY DEAR MOTHER,

Excuse this scrawl as the train is dancing.

I passed a good night and hope to have a good time all through. With all love for the sisters and Mr. [Clarence] Woolley (Husband of Mrs. Hale's daughter Harriet.) and Bud and Father Pope.

With love,

VIVEKANANDA

CLVII

To Sister Nivedita

THE CALIFORNIA LIMITED

SANTA FE ROUTE

December 2nd, 1899

MY DEAR MARGOT,

Two nights are passed — today the third will come. If it proves as pleasant and somnolent as the last two, I [shall] rejoice.

The scenery today I am passing through is much like the neighborhood of Delhi, the beginning of a big desert, bleak hills, scanty, thorny shrubs, very little water. The little streams are frozen, but during the middle of the day it is hot. Must be [illegible] I presume, in summer.

I send this to the care of Mrs. Adams, (Probably Mrs. Milward Adams.) as I don't know your address. The Chicago work will not give you much, I am sure, except in education in the methods here, which I am sure will work out soon.

With all love and blessings,

VIVEKANANDA

CLVIII

To Mrs. G. W. Hale

LOS ANGELES

6 December 1899

MY DEAR MOTHER,

A few lines to say my safe arrival and am going to resume my usual work of lecturing here.

I am much better than I was in Chicago and hope soon to become well again.

I cannot tell you how I enjoyed once more the little visit with my American Mother and Sisters.

Harriet has scored a triumph really. I am charmed with Mr. Woolley — only hope Mary will be equally fortunate. It gives me a new lease of life to see people happy. May they all be happy.

Ever with love, your son,

VIVEKANANDA

CLIX

To Sister Christine

921 WEST 21ST STREET,

LOS ANGELES,

9th December 1899.

MY DEAR CHRISTINA,

After all, it is good for me, and good for those I love, that I should come here. Here at last in California! One of our poets says: "Where is Benares, where is Kashmir, where Khorasan, where Gujarat! O Tulsi! thus, man's past Karma drags him on". And I am here. After all it is best, isn't it? Are you going to Boston? I am afraid you are not. I have not unsettled any of your plans, have I? — unnecessary expenses? Well, if any, I will make it up. Only the trouble is yours. I am ashamed of my eccentricities. Well, how are you? What are you doing? How are things going with you? Sleep if you can; it is better to sleep than get awakened. I pray that all good may come to thee — all peace, all strength to do and suffer. I have a great deal of strength to do, but very little to suffer.

I am so selfish again, always thinking of my own sufferings and paying no heed to others. Pray for me; send strong thoughts that I may have strength to suffer. I know you will. Now, I mean to remain a few weeks in this city. After that, "Mother" knows. I am physically much better now than I have been for months. The weakness of the heart is nearly gone. The dyspepsia is also much better, and [there is] very little. I can walk miles now without feeling it in the heart. If this continues, I expect to have a new lease on life. I am so, so sorry of asking you to come to Boston and flying away. If you are there, I hope you will enjoy the place and the meetings. If you have given it up — well, did you take leave and not go to Boston? My! what a bungle! Well, I ask a thousand pardons, if such is the case. Things must look brighter anyway, sooner or later. What of these little, few days of life!

How is Mrs. Funke? Loads of love for her. How long a leave [do] you get at Christmas? When does it begin? If you feel inclined and willing, write me a long note, will you? But don't tell my friends my whereabouts. I want to be off from the world for a time, if I can. Will you kindly send Mr. Freer's address to Mrs. Bull? She needs it. I had a lecture here last night. The hall was not crowded, as there was very little ad[vertisement], but a fairly good — sized audience though. I hope they were pleased. If I feel better, I am going to have classes in this city soon. I am on the business path this time, you know. Want a few dollars quick, if I can.

Ever yours in the Lord,

VIVEKANANDA.

CLX

To Swami Brahmananda

[Swami Vivekananda sent the following cablegram to his brother-monk.]

[Postmarked: December 13, 1899]

PERFECTLY CURED. BLESS ALL. VIVEKANANDA.

CLXI

To Sister Christine

921 WEST 21ST STREET,

LOS ANGELES,

27th December 1899.

DEAR CHRISTINA,

So you are awake and can't go to sleep any more. Good! Keep awake, wide awake. It was good I came here. For, in the first place, I am cured. What do you think of this — able to walk, and every day walk three miles after a heavy dinner! Good! Isn't it?

I am making money fast — twenty-five dollars a day now. Soon I will work more and get fifty dollars a day. In San Francisco I hope to do still better — where I go in two or three weeks. Good again — better, say I — as I am going to keep the money all to myself and not squander it any more. And then I will buy a little place in the Himalayas — a whole hill — about say, six thousand feet high with a grand view of the eternal snows. There must be springs and a tiny lake. Cedars — the Himalayan cedar forests — and flowers, flowers everywhere. I will have a little cottage; in the middle, my vegetable gardens, which I will work myself — and — and — and — my books — and see the face of man only once in a great while. And the world may go to ruin round about my ears, I would not care. I will have done with all my work — secular or spiritual — and retire. My! how restless I have been all my life! Born nomad. I don't know; this is the present vision. The future is to come yet. Curious —all my dreams about my own happiness are, as it were, bound to come to nothing; but about others' well-being — they as a rule prove true.

I am so glad you are happy and peaceful under Mrs. Bull's hospitable roof. She is a great, great woman — one whom to see is a pilgrimage.

No snow here — exactly like northern India in winter. Some days, even warmer — cool in the morning and evening, in the middle of the day, warm, in the sun, hot. The roses are about us, gardens everywhere, and the beautiful palms. But I like the snow: crisp, crackling under the feet, white, white, white — all round white!

I don't think I have anything with the kidneys or the heart. The whole thing was about indigestion and it is now nearly cured. A month more, and I will be strong like a lion and hardy like a mule. The poor English are getting it hot from the Boers. Mourning in every home in England and still the war goes on. Such is human folly. How long will it take for man to become civilized! Will wars ever cease? Mother knows! The New Year is sure to bring about a great change. Pray some good may come to India. I send you all joy, all love, all success for the New Year and many, many more to come.

So you did well, you think, by coming to Mrs. Bull. I am glad. I wanted you to know Mrs. Bull thoroughly. Remain there as long as you can. It will do you good, I am sure. Take heart and be of cheer, for next year is sure to bring many joys and a hundred blessings.

Yours truly,

VIVEKANANDA.

CLXII

To Sister Nivedita

LOS ANGELES

[Early February 1900]

DEAR MARGO [MARGOT],

You have the Gopâla. Add the Sâvitri story to that. I send you four more herewith. They ought to make a nice volume. Work on them a bit, will you. If you get a publisher in Chicago, all right; if not, Mr. Leggett promised to publish them sometime ago.

Yours,

VIVEKANANDA

P.S. The preliminary parts should be struck off.

CLXIII

To Miss Josephine MacLeod

1231 PINE STREET

SAN FRANCISCO.

March 2nd 1900

DEAR JOE —

Your note enclosing two from France and three from India just received. I have had general good news and am happy.

Financially, I have got $300 in Los Angeles. About Mrs. Bowler, she has about a hundred odd dollars in cash. Mrs. Hendrick and she have not paid up as yet. That money — $300 in all — is with her. She will send it to me whenever I write.

Rev. Benjamin Fay Mills, a very popular Unitarian preacher in Oakland, invited me from here and paid the fare to San Francisco. I have spoken twice in Oakland to 1500 people each time. Last time I got from collection $30. I am going to have classes at 50 cents admission each.

San Francisco had one lecture the other night [February 23] at 50¢ each. It paid its expenses. This Monday [Sunday?] I am going to speak free — after that a class.

I went to see Mrs. Hurst [Hearst]. She was not at home. I left a card — so with Prof. Le Conte.

Mary [Hale] writes that you wrote her of my coming any day to the East. I don't know. Here I have a large following —ready — made by my books. Will get some money, not much. St. Francis [Francis Leggett] may put the money in the bank for me — but can that be done without my signature? And I am here? It is good if it can be done. Did you see any possibility of my books being sold for good to any publisher?

The French invitation is all right. But it seems impossible to write any decent paper on the subject we chose. Because if I have to lecture and make money, very little time will be left for anything else. Again, I can not find any books (Sanskrit) here. So let me try to make a little money if I can and go to France all the same, but send them no paper. No scholarly work can be done in this haphazard and hurried fashion. It means time and study.

Shall I write to Mr. [Gerald] Nobel an acknowledgement and thanks? Write to me fully on these subjects if you can before you leave [for Europe]. My health is going on the same way. The gas is there more or less and this city is all climbing up[hill] — that tires me much.

With all love,

Yours affectionately,

VIVEKANANDA

P.S. Did anybody else respond to Mrs. Leggett's call?

CLXIV

To Sister Christine

1719 TURK STREET,

SAN FRANCISCO, CALIFORNIA,

12th March 1900.

DEAR CHRISTINA,

Just now received a letter from you through New York. I, the other day, wrote you one c/o Mrs. Funke, as I was not sure which of your addresses in my notebook was the correct one! Mental telepathy or foolishness — what is it?

By this time you must have got mine. There is nothing particular about me, except things are going on at the same rate — very little money — making, a good deal of work, and moving about. I leave here in April and come to Chicago for a few days, then to Detroit and then, through New York, go to England. I hope you are all right. I am very calm and peaceful mentally, and hope to remain so for the rest of my life.

How are Mrs. Funkey [Funke] and the rest of our friends?

With all love,

VIVEKANANDA.

CLXV

To Sister Christine

1719 TURK STREET,

SAN FRANCISCO,

[April 9, 1900]

Hello! What's the matter with you — gone to sleep? Have not had any news of you for a long time.

I am getting better every day, and one of these days — say in a few weeks — I am coming straight to say how-d'you-do. Well, I will be here two weeks more, then to a place called Stockton — thence to the East. I may stop a few days in Chicago. I may not.

Beginning of May, I come [for] sure to Detroit. I will, of course, write to you. How is life going on with you — grinding, as usual? Any improvements? Write a chatty letter if you feel like. I am dying to get news.

Ever yours in the Truth,

VIVEKANANDA.

CLXVI

To Sister Nivedita

C/O DR. LOGAN,

770 OAK STREET,

SAN FRANCISCO, CALIFORNIA,

17th May [1900].

DEAR MARGOT,

I am sorry, I cannot come to Chicago yet for a few days. The doctor (Dr. Logan) says I must not undertake a journey till completely strong. He is bent on making me strong. My stomach is very, very good and nerves fine. I am getting on. A few days more and I will be all right. I received your letter with the enclosed.

If you leave for New York soon, take my mail with you. I am coming to New York direct. If you leave New York before I leave, put my mail in a cover and deposit with Turiyananda, and tell him to keep it for me and not to open it on any account, nor any one of my Indian letters. Turiyananda will take charge. Also see that my clothes and books are at the Vedanta Society's rooms in New York.

I will write you more soon — an introduction to Mrs. Huntington. This affair should be private.

With love and blessings,

VIVEKANANDA.

P.S. As I have got to stop at Chicago for my ticket, will you ask anybody to take me in for a day or two, if Mrs. Hale is gone East by that time?

CLXVII

To Sister Nivedita

770 OAK STREET,

SAN FRANCISCO, CALIFORNIA,

18th May 1900.

DEAR MARGOT,

Enclosed find the letter of introduction to Mrs. Huntington. She can, if she likes, make your school a fact with one stroke of her pen. May Mother make her do it!

I am afraid I will have to go direct to New York, as by that time the Hales will be off. I cannot start for two weeks at least yet. Give the Hales my love.

With love and blessings,

Yours,

VIVEKANANDA.

P.S. I received your letter, including Yum's [Miss Josephine MacLeod's].

CLXVIII

To Mrs. Ole Bull (in London)

SAN FRANCISCO

18 May 1900

MY DEAR MOTHER,

Many thanks for Joe's [Miss Josephine MacLeod's] and your letters. I have again a bad relapse — and [am] struggling out of it. This time I am perfectly certain that with me all diseases are nervous. I want rest for two, three years — and not the least bit of work between. I will take rest with the Seviers in the Himalayas.

Mrs. [James Henry] Sevier gave me 6,000 Rs. for family — this was distributed between my cousin, aunt, etc. The 5,000 Rs. for buying the house was borrowed from the Math funds. Do not stop the remittance you send to my cousin, whatever Saradananda may say to the contrary. Of course I do not know what he says.

I have long given up the idea of a little house on the Ganges, as I have not the money.

But I have got some in Calcutta and some with the Leggetts, and if you give a thousand more, that will be a fund for my own personal expenses (as you know I never took Math money) as well as for my mother. Kindly write to Saradananda to give up the little house plan. I am not going to write any more for weeks yet — till I completely recover. I hope to get over [it] in a few weeks from now — it was a terrible relapse. I am with a Doctor friend [Dr. Milburn H. Logan], and he is taking every care of me.

Tell Joe that going amongst different people with a message also does not belong to the Sannyasin; for a Sannyasin, [there] is quiet and retirement, scarcely seeing the face of man.

I am now ripe for that, physically at least. If I don't go into retirement, nature will force me to it. Many thanks that temporal things have been so well arranged by you.

With all love to Joe and yourself —

Your Son,

VIVEKANANDA

CLXIX

To Sister Christine

C/O DR. LOGAN,

770 OAK STREET,

SAN FRANCISCO, CALIFORNIA,

19th May 1900.

DEAR CHRISTINA,

How are you? When is your vacation to commence? I am still in California. Hope to start for the East in two or three weeks more.

Write me all about yourself and how things are going on. How is Mrs. Funkey [Funke]? And the other friends?

Yours as ever,

VIVEKANANDA.

CLXX

To Swami Abhedananda

770 OAK STREET

SAN FRANCISCO, CAL.

C/O DR. LOGAN, M.D.

[May 19, 1900?]

MY DEAR ABHEDANANDA

I am very, very glad to hear about the new home of the Vedanta Society. As things stand, I will have to come to New York direct from here — without stoppage — but it will be two or three weeks yet, I am afraid. Things are coming up so fast that I can not but change my plans and stop a few more days.

I am trying my best to get one of you for a flying visit to this Coast — it is a great country for Vedanta.

Get all my books and clothes etc., in your home. I am coming soon. My love to Mrs. Crane. Is she still living on beef-steak and hot water? Miss [Sarah Ellen] Waldo and Mrs. Coulston write about the publication of a new edition of *Karma-Yoga*. I have written to Miss Waldo all about it. The money in hand from the sale of books ought to be spent, of course.

Do you see my books and clothes all safe there? They were with Mrs. Bull in Boston.

With all love,

VIVEKANANDA

CLXXI

To Sister Christine

VEDANTA SOCIETY,

102 EAST 58TH STREET,

NEW YORK,

9th June 1900.

DEAR CHRISTINA,

I could not write more, as the last few weeks of my stay in California was one more relapse and great suffering. However, I got one great benefit out of it inasmuch as I came to know I have really no disease, except worry and fear. My kidneys are as sound as any other healthy man's. All the symptoms of Bright's disease etc., are only brought on by nerves.

I wrote you one, however, from 770 Oak Street, San Francisco, to which I did not get any reply. Of course, I was bedridden then and my address book was not in the place I was in. There was a mistake in number. I cannot believe you did not reply willingly.

As you see, now I am in New York, and will be here a few days. I have an invitation from Mrs. Walton of Cleveland, Ohio. I have accepted it. She writes me you are also invited and have accepted her invitation. Well, we will meet in Cleveland then. I am sure to see you before I go to Europe — either there or anywhere you wish. If you don't think it would be possible for you to come to Ohio, I will come to any other place you want me to come to say goodbye.

When is your school going to close? Write me all about your plans — do!

Miss Noble wants me very much to go to Cleveland. I would be very, very glad to get a few weeks' seclusion and rest before I start with friends who do not disturb me at all. I know I will find rest and peace that way, and you can help me any amount in that. In Cleveland, of course, there will be a few friends always and much talkee-talkee as a matter of course. So if you think I will have real peace and rest elsewhere, just write all about it.

My reply to the Cleveland lady depends on your letter.

How I wish I were in Detroit or elsewhere just now, among friends who I know are good and true always. This is weakness; but when the physical vitality is lowered and the nerves all unstrung, I feel so, so much to depend upon somebody. You will be glad to learn I made a little money in the West. So I will be quite able to pay my expenses.

Write soon.

Yours affectionately,

VIVEKANANDA.

CLXXII

To Sister Christine

VEDANTA SOCIETY,

102 EAST 58TH STREET,

NEW YORK,

13th June 1900.

DEAR CHRISTINA,

There is no cause for any anxiety. As I wrote, I am healthier than ever; moreover, all the past fear of kidney troubles has passed away. "Worry" is the only disease I have, and I am conquering it fast.

I will be here a week or two, and then I come to Detroit. If things so happen that I cannot come, I will sure send for you. Anyway, I am not going to leave this country before seeing you. Sure, sure — I must see you first, and then go to Europe.

Things are looking cheerful once more, and good luck, like ill, also comes in bunches. So I am sure it will be smooth sailing every way now, for some time at least.

With love to Mrs. Funkey [Funke],

Ever yours in the Truth,

VIVEKANANDA.

CLXXIII

To Sister Christine

VEDANTA SOCIETY,

102 EAST 58TH STREET,

NEW YORK,

15th June 1900.

MY DEAR CHRISTINA,

I am getting better every day, only this New York is a bad place for sleep. Again, I am working some, though not hard, to get the old friends together and put the thing in shape.

Now, you know, I will in a week or so finish this work and then be ready for a real quiet of a week or two or more.

Detroit, alas! will be no better than New York. With so many old friends! How can you avoid friends whom you really love?

I will have perfect freedom at yours — sure — but how can I avoid seeing friends and the eternal visiting and paying visits and much talkee-talkee? Do you know any other place within eight or ten hours (I want to avoid night rides) of riding from New York where I can be quiet and free from the people? (Lord bless them.) I am dead tired seeing people just now. Just think of that and everything else; if, after all, you think Detroit is the best place for me, I am ready to come.

Yours truly,

VIVEKANANDA.

PS — I am also thinking of a quiet place.

CLXXIV

To Sister Christine

VEDANTA SOCIETY,

102 EAST 58TH STREET,

NEW YORK,

27th June 1900.

DEAR CHRISTINA,

This is my plan just now. I will have to remain in New York a few days yet to see my books through. I am going to publish another edition of *Karma-Yoga* and the London lectures in a book form. Miss Waldo is editing them, and Mr. Leggett will publish.

Then, I think, if I am to remain in this country a few weeks more, it is better that you get a rest and change. Newport is a celebrated seaside place — four hours from New York. I am invited there. I will go there this week and, as promised, I [will] find quiet and retirement and freedom. I will try to find a place for you and wire you as soon as found.

I am sure in Detroit you cannot have rest. A little change of place and quiet from time to time is a great factor in renewing one's vigour.

Well, if you think that you would have better rest and quiet in Detroit, drop a line and I come. It is only seventeen hours from New York to Detroit, and I am quite strong to undertake it. I am free to go already; only I really want you to take a good, long rest for some weeks at least.

Don't be afraid of expenses. Mother has amply provided that and will provide, so long I am unselfish.

Think [over] all the pros and cons, and write at your earliest convenience.

I am going to Newport anyway, just to see what it looks like. I will write you all about [it] as soon as I am there.

Ever yours in the Lord,

VIVEKANANDA.

CLXXV

To Mrs. Alice (Shanti) Hansbrough

THE VEDANTA SOCIETY,

102 EAST 58TH STREET, NEW YORK, N.Y.

[End of June 1900]

DEAR MRS. HANSBROUGH —

I have not written you a line since you left San Francisco. I am well and things are going on well with me.

I am in New York once more, where they have got now a home for the Society and their headquarters. I and the other Swamis also live there.

A San Francisco lady [Miss Minnie C. Boock] now here owns a plot of land near Mt. Hamilton, 12 miles east of Lick observatory — 160 acres in area. She is going to make us a present of it. It would be nice for a summer gathering for us in California. If friends like to go there *now*, I will send them the written authority. Will you write to Mrs. Aspinall and Miss Bell etc., about it? I am rather desirous it should be occupied this summer as soon as possible. There is only a log cabin on the land; for the rest they must have tents.

I am sorry I can not spare a Swami yet.

With all love to you and Mrs. [Carrie Mead] Wyckoff and the baby of the family.

Ever yours in the Truth,

VIVEKANANDA

P.S. Tell Helen [the youngest Mead sister] — I thank her for her kind invitation, but [am] so sorry [I] can not accept it now. After all, you three sisters have become a part of my mind forever. What about the club?

CLXXVI

To Sister Christine

[On July 3, 1900, before departing for Detroit with Swami Turiyananda and Miss Minnie Boock, Swami Vivekananda dispatched a telegram.]

[POSTMARKED: NEW YORK

July 3, 1900]

STARTED REACH TOMORROW Wednesday 2 P.M. COME STATION WABASH.

SWAMI VIVEKANANDA

CLXXVII

To Mrs. Alice (Shanti) Hansbrough

102 E. 58TH STREET,

NEW YORK,

3rd July 1900.

MY DEAR MRS. HANSBROUGH —

This is to introduce Swami Turiyananda. The lady who gave the piece of land for Vedanta work belongs to Los Angeles. She has taken Turiyananda with her. He is a great spiritual teacher — but has no experience in platform work.

The best thing would be to help him to start a centre for quiet and rest and meditation in the land near San Jose.

With all love to the holy Trinity.

Ever yours in the Lord,

VIVEKANANDA

CLXXVIII

To Swami Abhedananda

102 E. 58TH STREET,

NEW YORK,

24 July 1900.

DEAR ABHEDANANDA,

I would have gladly remained here, but *sastây kisti mât*. Got a fine berth — one room all to myself — on a fine vessel. As soon as August comes it will be a terrible Bhida [crowd] as the companies are reducing prices.

Things are going quite all right. Mr. Johnson has returned to their house, and all the rooms are full except two. You write to Mrs. Crane whether you want to get them or not.

You need not feel the least anxiety about the N.Y. work; it will go as a marriage bull next season. Give my love to Mrs. [Mary B.] Coulston and explain to her the circumstances.

With all love,

VIVEKANANDA

CLXXIX

To Sister Christine

A BORD DE PAQUEBOT LA CHAMPAGNE,

Friday morning, 9 a.m.,

3rd August 1900.

DEAR CHRISTINA,

It is foggy this morning. We are in the channel – expect to reach [Le Havre] at 12 a.m. [noon]. It has been a very bad voyage – rolling and raining and dark nearly all the time. Terrible rolling all through. Only last night I had good sleep. On other occasions the rolling makes me sleep well, but this time I don't know what was the matter; the mind was so whirling. Anyway, I am well and soon to reach land.

Hope to reach Paris this evening.

I send this to Detroit, expecting you there.

With all love and blessings,

VIVEKANANDA.

CLXXX

To Mrs. Francis Leggett

[Swami Vivekananda sent the following telegram on Friday, August 3, 1900, when the S.S. Champagne (which he had boarded in New York on July 26) docked at Le Havre, France.]

[Postmarked: Friday, August 3, 1900]

ARRIVE A HUIT HRES STLAZARE – VIVEKANANDA

[Translation: "I arrive at eight o'clock (p.m.) St. Lazare – VIVEKANANDA".]

CLXXXI

To Sister Christine

6, PLACE DES ETATS-UNIS

14th August 1900

DEAR CHRISTINE,

Your letter from New York reached just now. You must have got mine from France, directed to 528 Congress.

Well — it was a dreary, funeral-like time. Just think what it is to a morbid man like me!

I am going to the Exposition, etc., trying to pass time. Had a lecture here. Père Haycinth [Hyacinthe], the celebrated clergy — man here, seems to like me much. Well, well what? Nothing. Only, you are so good, and I am a morbid fool — that is all about it. But "Mother" — She knows best. I have served Her through weal or woe. Thy will be done. Well, I have news of my lost brother [Mahendranath Datta]. He is a great traveller, that is good. So you see, the cloud is lifting slowly. My love to your mother and sister and to Mrs. Funkey [Funke].

With love,

VIVEKANANDA

CLXXXII

To Sister Nivedita

6, PLACE DES ETATS UNIS,

PARIS,

23rd August 1900.

DEAR NIVEDITA,

The manuscript accounts of the Math just reached. It is delightful reading. I am so pleased with it.

I am going to print a thousand or more to be distributed in England, America and India. I will only add a begging paragraph in the end.

What do you think the cost will be?

With love to you and Mrs. Bull,

VIVEKANANDA.

CLXXXIII

To Sister Christine

6, PLACE DES ETATS-UNIS, PARIS

23rd August 1900

DEAR CHRISTINE,

What is the matter with you? Are you ill? Unhappy? What makes you silent? I had only one little note from you in all this time.

I am getting a bit nervous about you — not much. Otherwise I am enjoying this city. Did Mrs. A. P. Huntington write you?

I am well — keeping well as far as it is possible with me.

With love,

VIVEKANANDA

CLXXXIV

To Sister Christine

6 PLACE DES ETATS UNIS,

PARIS,

15th September 1900.

DEAR CHRISTINA,

Your letter was very reassuring. I am so glad this summer did you good. So you did not get enamoured of New York City.

Well, I am getting enamoured of Paris. I now am living with a M. Jules Bois, a French savant, who has been a student and admirer of my works.

He talks very little English; in consequence, I have to trot out my jargon French and am succeeding well, he says. I can now understand if he will talk slowly.

Day after tomorrow I go to Bretagne [Brittany] where our American friends are enjoying the sea breeze — and the massage.

I go with M. Bois for a short visit; *après cet* [after that] I don't know where I go. I am getting quite Frenchy, *connaissezvous* [do you know]? I am also studying *grammaire* and hard at work. [Sentence torn off] In a few months I hope to be Frenchy, but by that time I will forget it by staying in England.

I am strong, well and content — no morbidity.

Au revoir,

VIVEKANANDA.

CLXXXV

To Mrs. Ole Bull

66, RUE AMPERE

22nd October 1900

DEAR MOTHER,

I am sorry to learn you are not well. Hope you will soon be better. Things seem to turn out better for me.

Mr. Maxim of the gun fame is very much interested in me, and he wants to put in his book on China and the Chinese something about my work in America. I have not any documents with me; if you have, kindly give them to him. He will come to see you and talk it over with you. Canon Hawes [Reverend Hugh Reginald Haweis] also keeps track of my work in England. So much about that. It may be that Mother will now work up my original plan of international work. In that case, you will find your work of the Conference has not been in vain.

It seems that after this fall in my health, physical and mental, it is going to open out that way — larger and more international work. Mother knows best.

My whole life has been divided into successive depressions and rises — and so, I believe, is the life of everyone. I am glad, rather than not, these falls come. I understand it all; still, I suffer and grumble and rage!! Perhaps that is a part of the cause of the next upheaval.

I think you will be in America by the time we return; if not, I will see you in London again. Anyhow, adieu for the present. We start day after tomorrow for Egypt etc. And all blessings ever be on you and yours is, as always, my prayer.

Your son,

VIVEKANANDA

PS: To Margot [Sister Nivedita] my love, and I am sure she will succeed.

CLXXXVI

To Miss Alberta Sturges

[Swami Vivekananda sent the following postcard.]

[CONSTANTINOPLE,

November 1, 1900]

DEAR ALBERTA,

How are you? I am having a grand Turkish time.

Yours,

VIVEKANANDA

CLXXXVII

To Sister Christine

[On a postcard, picturing the old decayed fortress walls of Istanbul, Swami Vivekananda wrote the following note.]

[Postmarked: November 1, 1900]

DEAR CHRISTINA —

I am having a good time here. So I hope you also are having in Detroit —

Yours truly,

VIVEKANANDA.

CLXXXVIII

To Sister Nivedita

[On a picture postcard showing dervishes and local fish merchants, Swami Vivekananda wrote the following note.]

[POSTMARKED: CONSTANTINOPLE

November 1, 1900]

Dear Margo [Margot], the blessings of the howling dervishes go with you — Yours in the Lord,

VIVEKANANDA.

P.S. All love to Mrs. Bull.

CLXXXIX

To Sister Christine

[On a postcard, showing the temple of Hepaistos, popularly called Thesion, Swami Vivekananda wrote.]

[POSTMARKED: ATHENS,

November 11, 1900]

Great fun. I write without the possibility of being written to, as I am changing place all the time. How do you do?

VIVEKANANDA

CXC

To Maharaja Ajit Singh, the Raja of Khetri

THE MATH

BELOOR

HOWRAH DIST.

[December 1900]

YOUR HIGHNESS –

Very glad to learn that you and the Coomar [the Royal Prince] are enjoying good health. As for me, my heart has become very weak. Change, I do not think, will do me any good, as for the last 14 years I do not remember to have stopped at one place for three months at a stretch. On the other hand, if by some chance I can live for months in one place, I hope it will do me good. I do not mind this, however; I feel that my work in this life is done. Through good and evil, pain and pleasure, my life-boat has been dragged on. The one great lesson I was taught is that life is misery, nothing but misery. Mother knows what is best. Each one of us is in the hands of Karma – it works out itself, and no nay. There is only one element in life which is worth having at any cost – and it is love. Love immense and infinite, broad as the sky and deep as the ocean. This is the one great gain in life. Blessed is he who gets it.

Ever yours in the Lord,

VIVEKANANDA

CXCI

To Mrs. Ole Bull (in London)

DACCA,

20 March 1901.

MY DEAR MOTHER,

At last I am in Eastern Bengal. This is the first time I am here, and never before knew Bengal was so beautiful. You ought to have seen the rivers here — regular rolling oceans of fresh water, and everything so green — continual production. The villages are the cleanest and prettiest in all India.

Joe [Miss Josephine MacLeod] is perhaps by this time in Japan. I received a long and beautiful letter from Margot. Tell Margot that there has been of late a regular fall of fortune on the Kashmir Raja; things are all changing to his benefit. Mr. Mookherjey is now Governor of Kashmir. Saradananda had a bad fever. He is well now, but weak. He possibly goes to Darjeeling for a change. Mrs. [M. N.] Banerjey, who is at Calcutta, is very anxious to take him to the hills. Mohin [Mahendranath Datta], my brother, is in India, in Karachi near Bombay, and he corresponds with Saradananda. He writes to say he is going to Burma, China, etc. The traders who lure him have shops in all those places. I am not at all anxious about him. He is a very selfish man.

I have no news from Detroit. I received one letter from Christina nine months ago, but I did not reply. Perhaps that may have vexed her.

I am peaceful and calm — and am finding every day the old begging and trudging life is the best for me after all.

Mrs. Sevier I left at Belur. She is the guest of Mrs. Banerjey, who has rented Nilambar Mookherjey's house on the river (the old Math). She goes very soon to Europe.

Things are going on, as is in the nature of things. To me has come resignation.

With all love,

Ever your Son,

VIVEKANANDA.

PS — All blessings on Margot's work. Mother is leading, I am sure.

CXCII

To Ramesh Chandra Dutta

THE MATH, P.O. BELUR,

DIST. HOWRAH, BENGAL,

4 April 1901.

DEAR SIR,

I am so very glad to learn from a person of your authority of the good work Sister Nivedita is doing in England. I join in earnest prayer with the hopes you entertain of her future services to India by her pen.

I have not the least desire that she should leave her present field of utility and come over to India.

I am under a deep debt of gratitude to you, Sir, for your befriending my child, and hope you will never cease to advise her as to the length of her stay in England and the line of work she ought to undertake.

Her book on Kâli has been very popular in India. The debt our Motherland already owes you is immense, and we are anxiously awaiting the new book of yours.

May all blessings ever attend you and yours is the constant prayer of —

Yours humbly,

VIVEKANANDA.

CXCIII

To Sister Nivedita

THE MATH, BELUR,

HOWRAH DISTRICT, BENGAL,

4 April 1901.

DEAR MARGOT,

A letter came just now from Mr. R. Dutt [Ramesh Dutta] praising you and your work in England very much and asking me to wish you to stop longer in England.

It requires no imagination to learn that I am overjoyed at all the news about you Mr. Dutt so kindly sends.

Of course, you stay as long as you think you are working well. Yum [Miss Josephine MacLeod] had some talk about you with Mother [Holy Mother, Sarada Devi], and she desired you to come over. Of course, it was only her love and anxiety to see you — that was all; but poor Yum has been much too serious for once, and hence all these letters. However, I am glad it should happen, as I learnt so much about your work from Mr. Dutt, who can't be accused of a relative's blind love.

I have written to Mrs. Bull already about this matter. I am now at last in Dacca and had some lectures here. I depart for Chandranath tomorrow, near Chittagong, the farthest eastern extremity of Bengal. My Mother, aunt, cousin, another cousin's widow, and nine boys are with me. They all send you love.

I had just now a few lines from Mrs. Bull, also a letter from Mr. Sturdy. As it would be almost impossible for me to write for some days now, I ask you to thank Mrs. Bull for me for her letter, and tell her kindly that I have just now a long letter from Miss [Christina] Greenstidel of Detroit. She mentions a beautiful letter from Mrs. Bull. Sturdy writes about the publication of any further edition of *Raja-Yoga* by Longmans. I leave that consideration with Mrs. Bull. She may talk over the matter with Sturdy and do what she thinks proper.

Please give Sturdy my best love, and tell him I am on the march and will take time to reply to his letter; in the meanwhile the business will be looked after by Mrs. Bull.

With everlasting love and blessings,

VIVEKANANDA.

CXCIV

To Sister Christine

THE MATH, BELUR,

HOWRAH DIST., BENGAL,

[April 4, 1901]

DEAR CHRISTINE,

The subsequent proceedings have been so much interesting; and the interest has been growing so rapidly of late, that one could scarcely utter a word.

I am glad to learn of Mrs. [Ole] Bull's sweet letter to you; she is an angel. You are peaceful and happy — good. I am growing towards it too.

I am en route to Chandranath on pilgrimage.

I have been anxiously awaiting a letter from you, and it seemed it would never come.

I am sure to be happy — can't help thinking so. After so much struggle, the result must come. Things take their own course; it is I who am to brighten up, I find. And I am trying my best. And you can help me by writing nice letters now and then; will you?

Margot [Sister Nivedita] is doing splendid work in England with Mrs. Bull's backing. Things are going on nicely.

I am sleeping better and the general health is not bad.

With everlasting love and blessings,

VIVEKANANDA.

P.S. Please enquire of Miss [Sarah Ellen] Waldo about the publication of *Karma* and *Jnâna Yogas* and write.

CXCV

Letter of Introduction

GAUHATI

April 17, 1901

I have great pleasure in certifying the great amiability and helpfulness of the brothers Shivakanta and Lakshmikanta, Pandas of Shri Kamakhya Peetham.

They are men who help most and are satisfied with the least.

I can unhesitatingly recommend them to the Hindu public visiting this most holy shrine.

SWAMI VIVEKANANDA

CXCVI

To Sister Christine

THE MATH, BELUR,

HOWRAH DIST., BENGAL,

13th May 1901.

DEAR CHRISTINE,

I arrived in the Math yesterday. This morning came your short note. You must have got my letters by this time, and [I] hope this will give you a taste of how sometimes silence is gold.

I have beautiful letters from everywhere this morning and am quite happy. I paid a long visit of two months to Assam and different parts of eastern Bengal. For combined mountain and water scenery, this part of the country is unrivalled.

Either I am to go to Europe this summer, and thence to the U.S., or you come over to India — things are all getting ready to that end. Mother knows Her ways. For one thing, I am calm, very calm, and hope to keep a hold on this state for a long time; and you are my best help to keep this poise, are you not? I will write more in my next; just now these few lines — and a hundred pardons I beg for their scantiness. Yet silence tells more sometimes than all the speech in the world.

With all love and blessings,

Ever yours in the Lord,

VIVEKANANDA.

CXCVII

To Mrs. Ole Bull

THE MATH, BELUR

13 May 1901

DEAR MOTHER,

I reached Calcutta yesterday. This morning arrived your letter containing three cheques for my cousin. They shall reach her regularly.

I have not had any letter from Joe [Miss Josephine MacLeod] from Japan, but several I find awaiting me from on board steamer. She also sends me a newspaper cutting to be sent to Professor Geddes. I enclose it in this letter and expect you to direct it to Prof. Geddes.

Saradananda has been three weeks in Darjeeling, where he has improved greatly. I wish he will remain some time longer there. Mr. Bannerjy is the kindest of hosts.

Mrs. Sevier is in London at 2, Maisemore Mansions, Canfield Gardens, London, N.W.

You are right: my experiences are bringing about calmness — great calmness.

Mrs. Patterson and children are off to Europe. General [C. B. Patterson] is alone and very desirous that I would call. I will the next time I go to town.

My cousin and mother and the rest send love, and my eternal love you know always.

Ever your son,

VIVEKANANDA

P.S. All love and blessings for Margot [Sister Nivedita].

CXCVIII

To Mrs. Alice (Shanti) Hansbrough

THE MATH

HOWRAH DIST.,

BENGAL, INDIA

3rd June 1901

DEAR MRS. HANSBROUGH –

The contribution of six pounds and three shillings to the Math by the Los Angeles club has duly reached. Swami Brahmananda will write to you a separate acknowledgement. But as I happen to be here just now and have not had long any direct communication with you, I feel like having a chat with you as of yore, even though it be through the post. Now how are you and the Baby and the holy Trinity and the oldest who brings up the rear?

How are all our Los Angeles friends? Poor Mrs. [Emeline F.] Bowler, I hear, has passed away. She was an angel. Where is Miss Strickney? Please tender her my sincerest love, gratitude and prayers when you meet her next.

How are all the San Francisco friends? How is our Madam (Mrs. Benjamin Aspinall.) – the noble, the unselfish? What is she doing now? Quietly gone back to her Home of Truth work?

Are you pleased with Turiyananda and his work? Is the [Shanti] Ashrama progressing?

With everlasting love and blessings,

Ever yours in the Lord,

VIVEKANANDA

CXCIX

To Mr. Okakura Kakuzo

THE MATH, BELUR

HOWRAH DIS.

BENGAL, INDIA

18th June 1901

DEAR FRIEND —

Allow me to call you a friend. We must have been such in some past birth. Your cheque for 300 rupees duly reached and many thanks for the same.

I am just thinking of going to Japan, but with one thing or another and my precarious health, I cannot expedite matters as I wish.

Japan to me is a dream — so beautiful that it haunts one all his life.

With all love and blessings,

VIVEKANANDA

Kakudzo [Kakuzo] Okakura Esq.

Tokyo, Japan

CC

To Sister Christine

THE MATH, BELUR
DIST. HOWRAH, BENGAL, INDIA,
[End of June 1901]
DEAR CHRISTINA,

Your very welcome letter just reached. A few days ago a precious little bit of poem also reached. I wish it ever so much you were the writer thereof. Anyhow, most of us feel, though unable to express; and then, "There are thoughts that lie too deep for tears". Regularity in anything is not in my line of life, but that need not make you irregular. I pray you to drop a few lines every now and then. Of course, when I am not in this body, I am sure the news will reach you, and then you will have to stop writing.

Miss MacLeod wishes me to join her in Japan, but I am not sure. Most probably I am not going, especially as I expect both her and Mrs. Ole Bull in India, in November. Two whole months consumed in coming and going; only one month's stay in Japan — that does not pay, I am afraid.

Say, I am getting enormously fat about the middle — alas!

Mrs. [Charlotte] Sevier, who is now in England, returns in a few months to India. She has invited Mrs. Bull etc. to be her guests in the Himalayas. I wish they could be there during summer.

I have manfully borne the terrific heat of my country in the plains, and now I am facing the deluging rains of my country. Do you know how I am taking rest? I have got a few goats and sheep and cows and dogs and cranes! And I am taking care of them the whole day! It is not trying to be happy; what for? Why should one not be unhappy as well — both being nonsense? — but just to kill time.

Do you correspond with Mrs. Bull or Nivedita?

Don't worry, don't be anxious; for me the "Mother" is my protection and refuge; and everything must come round soon, better than my fondest dreams can paint.

With all love,

VIVEKANANDA.

CCI

To Sister Christine

THE MATH, BELUR,

DIST. HOWRAH, BENGAL,

6th August 1901.

Letters are sometimes, dear Christina, like mercy — good to the one that sends and the other that receives.

I am so happy that you are calm and resigned as ever. You are ever that. "Mother knows", indeed; only I know that "Mother" not only knows, but does — and is going to do something very fine for me in the near future. What do you think will be very good for me on earth? Silver? Gold? Pooh! I have got something infinitely better; but a little gold will not be amiss to keep my jewel in proper surroundings, and it is coming, don't you think so?

I am a man who frets much, but waits all the same; and the apple comes to my mouth by itself. So, it is coming, coming, coming.

Now, how are you? Growing ever thinner, thinner, thinner, eh? Do have a very good appetite and good sleep in anticipation of the coming good time — to be in trim for welcoming its advent.

How did the heat feel this year? We read all sorts of horrible stories about American heat waves. You have beaten the world's records, even in heat — that's Yankee push, surely.

Well, you are right as about taste: I renounce the yellow of gold and the white of silver, but stick to amber always — that is to my taste.

Amber and corals I always hated; but of late I am awakening to their beauty. One learns as he lives, is it not?

I am going to Darjeeling tomorrow for a few days and will write to you from there. Now *gute Nacht* [good night] and *au revoir* [good-bye] for the present.

Ever yours truly,

VIVEKANANDA.

CCII

To Sister Christine

THE MATH, BELUR,

DIST. HOWRAH, BENGAL,

27th August 1901.

DEAR CHRISTINE,

I am expecting a long, long letter from you; and, like all expectations of mine, [it] will not be realized, I fear.

Well, I need not bother you with the usual string of questions: How are you? What are you doing all this summer? etc. I am sure the Mother will [do] so much as to keep you in good health at least.

Now, Christina, for many reasons this letter happens to be short, very. It is written with the special purpose that as soon as you get this, send me your latest photograph.

Did you write to Miss [Sarah Ellen] Waldo about the publication of the books? I get no news and, what is more important, no money (that is between you and me) from the sale.

Did you have any news of Margot [Sister Nivedita], of Mrs. [Ole] Bull etc.? And are you happy? I sometimes feel I am, other times it is clouded. Well, it is all the body, after all — material. Goodbye.

Yours with love and blessings,

VIVEKANANDA.

PS — Do send the photo as soon as possible.

CCIII

To Sister Christine

THE MATH, BELUR,

DIST. HOWRAH, BENGAL,

2nd September 1901.

MY DEAR CHRISTINE,

I have been looking at one of your old photos — the only one you sent four or five years ago; and then I remember how changed and reduced you looked last summer; and it came to me that you must be awfully thin now, as it seems very hard for you to get rid of anxieties. This is simply foolish. Things will, of course, take their shape. We only make ourselves miserable by moping. It is very hard to manipulate one's philosophy to contribute to one's daily need. So it is with you, as with me. But it is easiest to take the teacher's chair and read a lecture. And that has been my life's business!! Indeed, that is the reason why there are more disciples up to the mark than teachers. The upshot of all this is that you must create a huge appetite, then gorge, then sleep and grow fat, fat, fat. Plump is the English word, is it not?

As for me, I am very happy. Of course, Bengal brings the asthma now and then, but it is getting tame, and the terrible things — Bright's disease and diabetes — have disappeared altogether. Life in any dry climate will stop the asthma completely, I am sure. I get reduced, of course, during a fit, but then it takes me no time to lay on a few layers of fat. I have a lot of cows, goats, a few sheep, dogs, geese, ducks, one tame gazelle, and very soon I am going to have some milk buffaloes. These are not your American bison, but huge things — hairless, half-aquatic in habits, and [that] give an enormous quantity of very rich milk.

Within the last few months, I got two fits [of asthma] by going to two of the dampest hill stations in Bengal — Shillong and Darjeeling. I am not going to try the Bengalee mountains any more.

Mrs. Bull and Nivedita are in Norway. I don't know when they [will] come over to India. Miss MacLeod is in Japan. I have not heard from her [for] a long while. They all are expected here in November, and will have a "hot time in this old town" etc. I pray you can come, and the Mother will open the door for it. I cannot but say my prayers mostly have been heard, up to date.

Well now, Christina, send me one of your latest photos next mail, will you? I want to see how much of fat you have accumulated in one year.

Anyhow, I will have to go to America with Mrs. Bull, I am sure. [Excision] By the by, *excusez-moi*, our Calcutta is never so hot as your Detroit or New York, with its added advantage — we are not required by our society to wear many things. The old Greeks used to think that wearing too many clothes and [feeling] shame to show any part of the body a peculiarity of barbarians! So the Hindus think, down to the present day. We are the most scantily clothed people in the whole world. Bless the Lord! How one would live otherwise in our climate!

3rd September —

I left the letter unfinished last night. The foreign English mail starts day after tomorrow. So begin again. The moon is not up yet, but there is a sunless glow upon the river. Our mighty Ganges (She is indeed mighty now, during the rains) is splashing against the walls of the house. Numerous tiny boats are flitting up and down in the dark; they have come to fish for our shads, which come up the river this season.

How I wish you were here to taste our shads — one of the most delicate fish in the world. It is raining outside — pouring. But the moment this downpour ceases, I rain through every pore — it is so hot yet. My whole body is covered by big patches of prickly heat. Thank goodness there are no ladies about! If I had to cover myself in this state of things, I surely would go crazy.

I have also my theme, but I am not despondent. I am sure very soon to pan it out into a beautiful ecstasy [excision]. I am half crazy by nature; then my overtaxed nerves make me outrageous now and then. As a result I don't find anybody who would patiently bear with me! I am trying my best to make myself gentle as a lamb. I hope I shall succeed in some birth. You are so gentle. Sometimes I did frighten you very much, did I not, Christina? I wish I were as gentle as you are. Mother knows which is best.

I would not take any supper tonight, as I ate rather heartily of the aforesaid shad! Then I have to think, think, think on my theme; and some subjects I think best in bed because the whole is made clear to me in dream. Therefore, I am going to bed, and *gute Nacht, bon soir*, etc., etc. No, no, it is now about 10 a.m. in Detroit. Therefore, a very happy day to you. May all good realities reach you today while I am expecting dreams.

Ever yours with love and blessings,

VIVEKANANDA.

CCIV

To Sister Christine

THE MATH, BELUR,

DIST. HOWRAH, BENGAL,

25th September 1901.

DEAR CHRISTINE,

I could not write you last mail, excusez [excuse]. But I have been expecting one from you for a long time. Hope one will come this mail.

I am just thinking of going over to Japan, as Miss [Josephine] MacLeod is so insistent. Perhaps something will be done; who knows?

From Japan, of course, a peep into America seems inevitable.

Not much news of Mrs. [Ole] Bull or Margot [Sister Nivedita]. Margot is rested, well, and strong. She will come to India some day, perhaps. I am soon expecting Mrs. [Charlotte] Sevier though. Her work is needing her. Her beautiful home in the Himalayan forests is a temptation, especially now when a huge tiger is roaming in her compound and killed a horse, a buffalo, and her pair of mastiffs in broad daylight; a number of bears [are] playing havoc with her vegetable garden; and lots of porcupines [are] doing mischief everywhere!!! She went out of the way to buy land in a forest — she and her husband liked it so much.

There is not much to write this week. Words only tire one, except one which is inexhaustible, infinite.

So, goodbye till next week.

Ever with love and blessings,

VIVEKANANDA.

PS — Just now comes a telegram from Miss MacLeod and a letter also. She is so insistent that I am thinking of going over to Japan. In that case, we cross over to America this winter, and thence to England.

Yours,

CCV

To Sister Christine

THE MATH, BELUR,

DIST. HOWRAH, BENGAL,

8th October 1901.

DEAR CHRISTINA,

Yours of September 9 came to hand yesterday. I congratulate you on your successful visit to the Huron Lake; a few more of them (according to your letter) will force you to sympathize with our condition — oh, the gasping and the melting and the puffing and all the rest of them!

However, nothing in the world like a plump, ripe fruit.

I had to give up my trip to Japan: firstly, because I am not in a working trim yet; secondly, [I] don't much care to make such a long voyage (one month) alone; thirdly, what am I to talk to them, I wonder.

Our heat too has been fierce and is continuing unusually long this year. I am blacker than a Negro by this time.

The California work is progressing famously. They want one or two men more. I would send, if I could, but I have not any more spare men. Poor Turiyananda is suffering from malaria yet, and is awfully overworked.

Do you know whether they published my *Jnana-Yoga* or not? I got a copy of a second edition of *Karma-Yoga* only.

I am bobbing up and down in the current of life. Today it is rather down, so I finish the letter here.

Yours with all love and blessings,

VIVEKANANDA.

CCVI

To Sister Christine

THE MATH, BELUR,

DIST. HOWRAH, BENGAL,

14th October 1901.

MY DEAR CHRISTINA,

Just now came a letter from Mrs. Bull, but none from you, as I expected one this mail.

Mrs. Bull writes, "I wrote Christina recently to ask her if she were to be free in case the opportunity opened for her to go to the East. I send you her reply".

I went through several times your letter to Mrs. Bull. It surely was horrible; and you have been all this time hiding the real state of affairs from me and posing great cheerfulness!!

You will be a precious fool to lose the opportunity if such comes and is offered by Mrs. Bull. You will only have to take a year's leave. The rest will all be arranged by Mrs. Bull, including, I am sure, all your anxiety for those you will have to leave behind in Detroit.

You have been good, too good to be human, and you are so, still. But it is no use making oneself unnecessarily miserable. "Mother's will", surely, if the chance comes; and it has got to come, I know.

I would not write you about my health; for after all this hide and seek, even though it was for my good, I think you have not much of a right to know the truth about my health.

But to some things you have eternal rights, and amongst others, to my eternal love and blessings,

VIVEKANANDA.

CCVII

To Sister Nivedita

THE MATH,

P.O. BELUR, HOWRAH,

12th November 1901.

MY DEAR MARGO [MARGOT],

Since the Durgâ Pujâ I have been very ill, and so could not reply to your letter earlier.

We had a grand Puja here of Durga, lasting nearly four days; but, alas, I was down with fever all the time.

We had a grand image, and a huge Puja it was. Then we had the Lakshmi Puja following close, and then night before yesterday, we had the *Kali Puja*. It is always after midnight — this Puja. I am better now, and we will find a house for you as soon as you come.

I am so glad you are accompanying Mrs. [Ole] Bull. She requires all care; and she always thinks of herself the last. Joe [Miss Josephine MacLeod] is coming to India shortly — at Christmas time with some Japanese friends. I am expected to meet her in Madras.

I am going off to the N.W.P. [North-Western Provinces] etc. soon, as Bengal is malarious — now that the rains are over.

Mrs. Bull has been a mother to us all, and any time and service spent for her is as nothing to what she has been doing for us all. Remain with her as long as she wants you — the work can wait well; "Mother" sees to her work. We needn't be anxious.

By the by, Miss [Henrietta] Müller is here in Calcutta. She wrote a letter to Akhandananda, with whom she has been in regular correspondence — care of the Math. So I sent some flowers and fruits and a letter of welcome to her hotel. I have not had a reply yet.

Mrs. [Charlotte] Sevier, I expect, has already started. Swarupananda had his heart weakened by the constant uphill and downhill. He is here and improving.

Things are going on well with us, slowly but surely. The boys of late have been very active, and it is work only that tells and nothing else.

Yours with all love and blessings,

VIVEKANANDA.

CCVIII

To Sister Christine

THE MATH, P.O. BELUR, HOWRAH,

12th November 1901.

DEAR CHRISTINA,

The morning's mail brought me a photograph from Detroit. I thank the sender very much for promptness. Well, I liked it much. But the old one is the profile view; this, the front. Then again, the phenomenal fat seems to be only imaginary on somebody's part. In a way, I am more used to the old one, and, as such, I cannot slight an old friend. So let me say both are good. The one is an evolution of the other — for the better. I expected a line but it has not arrived yet; [it] may tomorrow. We have a proverb here: "One river is equal to forty miles". There is only a river between Calcutta and our Math, and yet such a round — about way for the mail. Sometimes it comes dribbling for days.

Mrs. [Ole] Bull and Nivedita must have started for the U.S. by this time. Nivedita is sure to see you in Detroit. Mrs. Bull is anxious to induce you to join her Indian party via Japan. If you can take leave for some months, do come. Mother will arrange anyhow; I need not trouble myself.

Mrs. Sevier has started already, it seems — alone.

We had grand Pujas (worships) here in our Math this year. The biggest of our Pujas is the Mother worship, lasting nearly four days and nights. We brought a clay image of Mother with ten hands, standing with one foot on a lion, the other on a demon. Her two daughters — the Goddess of Wealth and the Goddess of Learning and Music — on either side on lotuses; beneath, her two sons — the God of War and that of Wisdom.

Thousands of people were entertained, but I could not see the Puja, alas! I was down with high fever all the time. Day before yesterday, however, came the Puja of Kali. We had an image, too, and sacrificed a goat and burned a lot of fireworks. This night every Hindu home is illuminated, and the boys go crazy over fireworks. There are, of course, several cases of severe burns in the hospitals. We had less fireworks but more Puja, recitation of Mantras, offering of flowers, food and songs. It lasted only one night.

I am expected to leave Calcutta and Bengal in a few days, as this country becomes very malarious this month, after the rains. It is pleasant and cool now, and the north Himalayan wind is blowing.

We have fenced in a lot of our grounds to protect our vegetables from our cows and goats and sheep. The other day one of my [a portion excised] . . . but the mother was either so wicked or [a portion excised] . . . that she would not look at her young. I tried to keep them alive on cow's milk, but the poor things died in the night! Two of my ducks are sitting on their eggs. As this is their first time, and the male does not help them a bit, I am trying my best to keep up their strength by good feeding. We cannot keep chickens here — they are *forbidden* to us.

With all love,

VIVEKANANDA.

CCIX

To Sister Christine

THE MATH, P.O. BELUR, HOWRAH,

25th November 1901.

DEAR CHRISTINE,

It seems your bottle of nerve tonic did not do you much good, your assurances to the contrary. It must have been a curious error. I must have been down with fever or asthma or something else at that time. Still a thousand, thousand pardons. This was my first, and it will be my last, offence. Your letter that went to Miss [Josephine] MacLeod has not come back yet. Perhaps Miss MacLeod is bringing the letter with her, as she is coming over to India from Japan herself, accompanied by her Japanese converts (male, of course, as she is a lady missionary).

Well, well, I so wish things would so arrange themselves that I could see you once more. Mother knows. By the by, my right eye is failing me badly. I see very little with that one. It will be hard for me for some time either to read or write; and as it is getting worse every day, my people are urging me to go to Calcutta and consult a doctor. I will go soon, as soon as I recover from a bad cold I have on.

I am so glad you were so taken by Abhedananda; only I thought one Hindu was good for a lifetime.

Poor Miss Joe [Miss Josephine MacLeod] — so she remains ignorant as to the real cause of my not going over to Japan! You need not be the least anxious — there is no harm done; and if there were, Joe and especially Mrs. [Ole] Bull make it their life's duty to befriend those I love.

I will try your tonic when it arrives; and the gift, I pray, will even be followed by the giver, for surely a [words excised] . . . is more stimulating and healing than dead drugs.

With all love,

VIVEKANANDA.

CCX

To Sister Christine

THE MATH, P.O. BELUR, HOWRAH

27th November 1901.

DEAR CHRISTINE,

It is almost sure, I did not write any letter to you that week in which [I] made that infamous blunder. As I wrote you two letters a few days previously, it is not at all probable that I wrote you another. Then Miss [Josephine] MacLeod [would have] sent the letter back. I must have written only one letter that week to Miss MacLeod, giving her my reasons for not going to Japan; and somehow it so happened that the hand wrote the most familiar name on the envelope. So you need not expect any letter of yours back from Japan, as there was none; and if there were, you shall have it.

I am just under another spell of catarrh and asthma. Yesterday a cyclone blew over the place, and several trees and a bit of the roof are damaged. It is gloomy yet and cold. You know it is almost impossible to write with the asthma on. So *au revoir* [good-bye].

VIVEKANANDA.

CCXI

To Sister Christine

THE MATH, P.O. BELUR, HOWRAH

12th December 1901

DEAR CHRISTINE,

Well, then, you wanted to know all about my state of health, and you insist. You shall have it.

You know, the last three years I have been getting albuminuria now and then. It is not constant, nor is it yet of any organic character. The kidneys are structurally all right. Only they throw out albumen now and then.

This is worse than throwing out sugar in diabetes. Albumen poisons the blood, attacks the heart and does all sorts of mischief. Catching cold always increases it. This time it has caused a small blood vessel in the right eye to burst, so that I scarcely see with that eye.

Then the circulation has become very rapid. The doctors have put me to bed; and I am forbidden to eat meat, to walk or even stand up, to read and write.

Already there is some benefit in this lying-down process, as I sleep a lot and have a good appetite and am digesting my meals. Curious, is it not, that inactivity should bring on sleep and appetite? There is no cause to be anxious at all.

Mrs. [Charlotte] Sevier arrived in Calcutta three days ago; and by the last advice from Nivedita, Mrs. Bull and she will start on the 13th December, if they can secure berths, or on the 30th December at least. I pray Mrs. Bull has already invited you and that you have got your year's leave and are coming over, and that you will get this letter in India redirected. If Mother does not fulfil this prayer, sure She will take me across the water soon, and [line excised] . . . . The doctor says if I keep to my bed for three months, I will get completely cured.

Now, don't worry. If good days are not coming, we will make them, that is all. Hang it! I must have good days now and, that too, very soon. You know, I always keep my word. Mother must do it, or I throw Her overboard. I am not so submissive as you are.

Our old-school physicians pour in tons of iron and other metals — including gold, silver, pearls, etc. — down our throats. I should be a man of iron by this time; perhaps yours will be the last touch to make my body one of steel.

This is our best season for eating turtles, but they are all black. The green [ones] can only be found in America. Alas! I am prevented from the taste of meat.

Now, noble heart, take courage. Don't mope: you have buffeted [too] many a storm in life, old war horse, to be like a silly boarding-school girl. Things must go all right. I am not going to die or to be ill just now; I am determined to be healthy. You know my grit.

Miss [Josephine] MacLeod sent you your letter. What was it about? Was there anything queer? I am glad she had it. She writes beautifully about you. She has already started, and we will have a jolly good company this winter here in Calcutta. Mrs. [Ole] Bull, Miss MacLeod, Mrs. Sevier and Nivedita and I will be overjoyed if somebody else will be thrown into the bargain. I can't get any more value, eh? I must stop. Am going to look after my geese and ducks just for five minutes, breaking the doctor's command to lie down all the time. One of the geese is a silly, fearful bird, always despondent and anxious. She likes to be all alone by herself and is miserable — very much like another goose I know in another place.

Here my story ends
And spinach top bends.
Why is spinach withering?
Because the goat is browsing.
Why is the goat browsing?
Because no grass is growing.
Why no grass is growing?
The gardener is not watering.

Why there is no watering?
The Master is not commanding.
Why is he not commanding?
An ant has bitten the Master!

This is a nursery rhyme told after a story, and it is true of us all. It is only an ant bite, after all — the trouble here; is it not?

Ever yours,

VIVEKANANDA.

CCXII

To Sister Christine

THE MATH, BELUR,

DIST. HOWRAH, BENGAL, INDIA,

18th December 1901.

DEAR CHRISTINE,

I am much better, and the rest is doing me good. I have found out that lying in bed all the time gives me as much sleep as wanted and good digestion too. Albumen and sugar vanish immediately [when] I begin taking rest.

Mrs. Bull and Nivedita start for India from Marseilles today, and unless they change their plan, [they] must be in India before this reaches you — two weeks before.

Herewith I send you four hundred and eighty dollars by cheque drawn on Thomas Cook & Son, Broadway, New York. They have no branch office in Detroit. On receipt of this, you write to Thomas Cook & Son, Broadway, New York, that you have got a cheque from India — mentioning the amount and number — drawn by Thomas Cook & Son on the firm of Thomas Cook & Son, and want to be advised as to how to cash it. Don't send the cheque ahead. (Excuse all these details. I feel you are a baby in business, though I am worse.) This is to pay your "passage to India" if you think fit to accept Mrs. Sevier's invitation. If you get leave and come, I am sure you will find somebody who is coming to England, at least. Then from there, again, somebody who is coming to Egypt. You come with them as far as Italy, thence direct on a boat to India.

Second-class passage across the Atlantic is all right, but the second class from Italy to Bombay is rather bad. There are always a few rough men and fast women. There is money enough for travelling first class all through, if you so like.

The Mother will see to it, even as [She did when] this money came. Drop me a line as soon as you engage your passage —better a week ahead; otherwise I don't see how the letter can reach me. The vessel to India you get from London; and possibly a letter may reach me with the name of the vessel, etc. In any case, however, you wire me as soon as you land and get into a *good* hotel. You will find many persons to receive you — and me too, most probably.

In case, however, things take another turn and you cannot come, no matter. Do with the money just as it pleases you.

It is very probable that after Miss [Josephine] MacLeod and Mrs. [Ole] Bull have been through India, they are going home via Japan; and, of course, I am going with them. In that case I will be in California next fall.

It will be a nice trip, and would it not be a fine tour round the world if you get leave and come?

Do just as the Mother opens the way for you, and do not worry.

Yours with all love and blessings,

VIVEKANANDA

CCXIII

To Sister Christine

THE MATH, BELUR,

DIST. HOWRAH, BENGAL, INDIA,

25th December 1901.

A Merry Christmas and Happy New Year is the usual congratulation. Alas! The stars brought you a tremendous blow. (Sister Christine's mother had passed away.) Blessed be the name of the Lord. After all, it is only "Thy will be done" — our only refuge. I will not insult you by offering you consolation — you know it all already. Only this line to remind you of one who is in entire sympathy with you and who knows that all your plans must be good in joy or sorrow, as you are dedicated to the eternal Mother. Well, the Mother phenomenal has merged in the Mother absolute, eternal. Thy will be done.

By this time you must have made a decision, or, rather, the "Mother" has shown you the way, surely. I rest content.

The soldier of the Queen has gone abroad to fight for Her cause, leaving all he loves to Her care. The soldier is to look to his duty. The Queen of the Universe knows the rest.

With all love as usual,

VIVEKANANDA.

CCXIV

To Sister Christine

THE MATH, BELUR, DIST. HOWRAH,

23rd January 1902.

MY DEAR CHRISTINE,

By this time you must have settled your plans. Don't worry, however, on my account. I only want to see you rested and well rested, wherever you be.

Excuse this rather long delay in writing. Owing to various reasons I could not, but [was] mentally sending you good wishes all along.

Miss [Josephine] MacLeod has arrived with her Japanese friends: Mr. Okakura [Kakuzo], a professor of art, and Mr. Hori, a Brahmachârin. The latter has come to India to study Sanskrit and English. The former came to see India, the Motherland of Japanese culture and art. Well, Mrs. [Ole] Bull and Nivedita are also expected in a few days. As it seems now, this whole party is going to Japan — minus Nivedita. She remains here to work.

Now, I am going to try my hand in Japan and, if possible, in China. Oh, how I wish you were coming with Nivedita to make one of the party to Japan! Yet, do not put yourself to unnecessary trouble for that. There is Japan, and there is the U.S., after all, where we meet. You will only break yourself in trying to "hustle up". No Hurry, No Worry. I am rather anxious in not hearing from you for weeks. I pray you are not ill, anyway.

To Mother have I given you over. She protects Her own, ever and ever, I have no fear.

With all love and blessings,

VIVEKANANDA.

CCXV

To Miss Josephine MacLeod

GOPAL LAL VILLA, BENARAS CANTONMENT

7th Feb. 1902.

MY DEAR JOE —

We have safely reached Benaras, and Mr. Okakura [Kakuzo] has already done Benaras. He goes to see *Sarnath* (the old Buddhistic place) today and starts on his tour tomorrow.

He has asked Niranjan [Swami Niranjanananda] to accompany him and he has consented.

Kanay [Nirbhayananda] has supplied him with everything he asked for — and he asks me also to send you the accounts. This, on the other page.

I hope Nivedita and Mrs. [Ole] Bull have safely arrived. I am rather better than at Buddha Gaya. This house is nice — well furnished and has a good many rooms and parlours. There is a big garden all round and beautiful roses — and gigantic trees. It is rather cooler here than at Gaya. There was no hitch to our friends being admitted into the chief temple and [allowed to] touch the Sign of Shiva and to worship. The Buddhists, it seems, are always admitted.

With all love and welcome to Mrs. Bull and Nivedita — if they have arrived — and all to you,

VIVEKANANDA

[Enclosed in the above letter was the following accounts list.]

4TH FEBRUARY 1902. Rs 100

	Rs.	As.	P.*
Train hire from Gaya to Benares	20	4	0
Cab hire	5	0	0
Tel message	2	0	0

Refreshment Room (Morning)	1	8	0
Cooly hire Gaya	0	10	0
Tobacco etc.	0	5	0
Refreshment Room (Evening)	2	0	3
Cooly hire (at Benares)	1	1	0
Cab hire at Benares	1	10	0
Total	34	6	3

5TH FEBRUARY

Paid to Medicine for Mr. K. Okakura	1	8	0
" [Ditto] Oatmeal & corn — flour	1	4	0
" Tobacco etc.	0	6	3
" Bread etc.	0	2	0
Paid to Barber	0	3	0
" Fish	0	7	6
Total	3	14	9

6TH FEBRUARY 1902

Pickles	1	0	0
Sweetmeats	0	9	0
Carriage hire	1	8	0
Priests of Vishvanath etc.	10	4	0
Total	13	5	0

Things purchased for store at

Gopal Lal Villa before Swamiji's arrival	17	11	9
	------	------	------
Total	69	5	9
Paid to Expenses from Calcutta to Buddh—Gaya	30	10	3
	------	------	------
Rs.	100	0	0

("P." stands for pie-s, twelve of them making one Anna (As.) and sixteen annas making one rupee (Rs.).)

CCXVI

To Miss Josephine MacLeod

GOPAL LAL VILLA

BENARAS CANTONMENT

14 February 1902.

DEAR JOE —

I received a note yesterday from Mr. Okakura [Kakuzo]. They have seen Agra on their way to Gwalior. They must be there now.

The wire he sent to Japan was to Mr. [Tokuno] Oda to come immediately. There was a work. "Six" in it also.

It is quite cool here even now — and will remain so for this month at least. Is it getting warm in Calcutta?

I hope Mrs. [Ole] Bull and Nivedita are getting well rested after that tremendous journey.

I am so so.

The boys all send love.

Ever Yours with love and blessings,

VIVEKANANDA.

CCXVII

To Mrs. Alice (Shanti) Hansbrough

BENARAS

14 Feb. 1902

MY DEAR MRS. HANSBROUGH,

I am eternally indebted to you for what you did for me in the past, and infinitely more now for what you are doing for Turiyananda.

A gloom came over the Math when news reached Calcutta of his severe illness. Now, I hope, he has recovered completely, and I will be so glad to get the news from you.

It seems the American climate does not suit him. In that case it will be better for him to come over to India whenever he thinks fit.

In all probability I am going to Japan in a month or two. Ramakrishnananda accompanies me. Turiyananda may come over to Japan and I go to America. "Mother" knows best, however, and we obey.

I am just now in Benaras for a few days. All letters should, however, be addressed to the Belur Math.

Kindly convey my best love to Turiyananda and to yourself, the holy family and the other friends.

Ever yours in the Lord,

VIVEKANANDA

PS. Let Turiyananda take rest all the time now. He must not work at all till I reach Japan or America.

CCXVIII

To Sister Nivedita

GOPAL LAL VILLA,

BENARAS CANTONMENT,

4th March 1902.

MY DEAR MARGO [MARGOT],

It is night now, and I can hardly sit up or write, yet still feel duty bound to write to you this letter, fearing lest it becomes my last, it may put others to trouble.

My condition is not at all serious, but it may become [so] any time; and I don't know what is meant by a low fever that almost never leaves me and the difficulty of breathing.

Well, I sent Christina [Greenstidel] £100 from Mrs. [Charlotte] Sevier for a travel to India, as she lost her mother at that time. Her last letter informs me that she sails on February 15th. In that case, her reaching India is very near. I expect, of course, some information as to the port and steamer next week. In case I pass away, which I would like very much to do in this city of Shiva, do you open her letters directed to me, receive the girl, and send her back home. If she has no money to go back, give her a passage — even if you have to beg.

I have spent the little money I brought from Europe in feeding my mother and paying her debts. What little remains I cannot touch, as that is the expense for the pending lawsuit.

In case I rally, I will inform you of the time of her arrival, and, in that case, you will have to see that she comes in safe to some station in Bareilly, where I [will] meet her. And she is to be the guest of Mrs. [Charlotte] Sevier. I am also going to take another chance in Almora.

Ramakrishnananda came a few weeks before I came away, and the first thing he did was to lay down at my feet 400 Rs. he had collected in so many years of hard work!!! It was the first time such a thing has happened in my life. I can scarcely suppress my tears. Oh, Mother!! Mother! There is not all gratitude, all love, all manliness dead!!! And, dear child, one is enough — one seed is enough to reforest the world.

Well, that money is in deposit in the Math. I never mean to touch a penny of that. When I asked Ramakrishnananda to give that money to his people, he replied he did not care a hang to give to anybody except me and was only sorry he could scrape that little in four years! Well, if I pass away, see that 400 Rs. is paid back — every rupee to him. Lord bless you and Ramakrishnananda.

I am quite satisfied with my work. To have left two true souls is beyond the ambition of the greatest.

Ever your loving father,

VIVEKANANDA.

CCXIX

To Sister Christine

THE MATH, BELUR,

DIST. HOWRAH, BENGAL,

30th March 1902.

MY DEAR CHRISTINE,

You know how welcome you are — I need not express it. This is a land where expressions are studiously subdued. Margot [Sister Nivedita] and Joe [Miss Josephine MacLeod] have already written and made arrangements at Bombay. I expect and wait for you here in Calcutta. I wish I could be in Bombay to receive you, but all our wishes are not to be fulfilled.

Come over straight; only take great, great care of the heat by protecting the back of the head.

The trains here are not so safe as in your country, so have a little care of your things during night travel.

If you feel tired, take rest in Bombay. Mrs. [Ole] Bull, Joe and Margot are anxiously awaiting you, and so is

VIVEKANANDA.

CCXX

To Mrs. Ole Bull

[THE MATH, P.O. BELUR, DIST. HOWRAH,

March (?) 1902]

DEAR MOTHER,

I am glad Chinnu has arrived. Any hour you like will suit [me] for your coming tomorrow. But it is ferocious heat here from 11 a.m. to 5 p.m.

I would, therefore, suggest that you start after breakfast and remain the day here and have some Bengalee fish lunch, and go back in the evening.

I insist on your taking a cab here and back. A cab to come and go costs quite as much or less than a boat, and there is no change [of transportation]. If the cabby does not understand Belur, tell him to go to a place two miles south of Bally. He must know Bally, and then let him ask his way to the Math.

One such drenching and capsizing experience as Mr. Okakura [Kakuzo] had the other day will unsettle your nerves for days; and we expect such rough weather every evening this month. The land route is nearer, easier, and cheaper from where you are. I have also instructed your servant, the bearer of the letter.

Ever your Son,

VIVEKANANDA.

CCXXI

To Miss Josephine MacLeod

THE MATH

2nd April 1902

MY DEAR JOE —

The telegram is already gone, and I expect you will fill all arrangements there.

The Dak bungalows en route to Mayavati provide no food, nor have they cooks.

Provisions have to be taken at Kathgodam and arrangements made.

If you find any difficulty, go straight to Almora and make your arrangements at leisure. The Dak bungalows on the way to Almora provide food and in Almora there is a nice Dak bungalow.

Hoping everything will come your way, as it always does — (except Grandpa's health).

Yours affectionately,

VIVEKANANDA

I like Mr. [Tokuno] Oda much — he means business.

CCXXII

To Sister Christine

THE MATH, BELUR,

DIST. HOWRAH,

15th May 1902.

MY DEAR CHRISTINE,

So glad to learn you like Mayavati. The heat here has come in earnest, and no rain. I drink very little water though.

I have given up all idea of going to Mayavati or Almora. I bear the heat well, but the rains here are to be avoided. I will remove [myself] to somewhere else then.

No news from Calcutta. I am in a hurry. Write me the details of whatever you see or feel there — about men and things.

Yours with all love,

VIVEKANANDA.

CCXXIII

To Mme. Emma Calvé

[This letter of condolence was written upon the death of Mme. Calvé's father and enclosed in a letter to Miss Josephine MacLeod.]

THE MATH, BELUR

HOWRAH DISTRICT

BENGAL, INDIA

the 15th May 1902

MY DEAR MADEMOISELLE,

With great sorrow I learn the sad bereavement that has come upon you.

These blows must come upon us all. They are in the nature of things, yet they are so hard to bear.

The force of association makes out of this unreal world a reality; and the longer the company, the more real seems the shadow. But the day comes when the unreal goes to the unreal, and, ah, how sad to bear.

Yet that which is real, the Soul, is ever with us, omnipresent. Blessed is the person who has seen the real in this world of vanishing shadows.

I hope, dear Mademoiselle, you have greatly improved in health since our last meeting in Egypt.

May the Lord always shower His choicest blessings on you is the everlasting prayer of

VIVEKANANDA

CCXXIV

To Sister Christine

THE MATH, BELUR, DIST. HOWRAH,

27th May 1902.

MY DEAR CHRISTINE,

I am sorry I could not visit the mountains this time. My health, though not improved as much as I [had] wished, is not bad. The liver has been benefited — [that] is a great gain. The rains will commence very soon in the hills. So it is useless for me to take all the trouble of that terrible route.

I am so happy to learn the mountains are doing you good. Eat a lot, sleep as much as you can, and get plump. Stuff yourself till you get plump or you burst.

So the place did not suit Mr. Okakura [Kakuzo] — why? There must have been something to annoy him very much that he left the place so abruptly. Did he not like the scenery? Was it not sublime enough for him? Or the Japanese do not like sublimity at all? They only like beauty.

One of the boys writes that the little boy is getting disobedient etc. Mrs. Sevier wants me to take him down. So I do. I have asked Sadananda and another monk (whom I want for work here) to go to Almora and wait for the monsoon, and when it breaks, to come down.

If you feel you are becoming the least burdensome to Mrs. Sevier, write me immediately. It would be a sin to put further pressure on her — she does so much for me. However, she likes you very much and writes that you look be-au-ti-ful in saris.

I have just now two kids and three lambs added to the family. There was one more kid, but he got himself drowned in the yellow fish tank. How is Margot? Is she still there, or gone away with Mr. Okakura? How is she pulling on with the boys?

What do you do the whole day? How do you pass the day? Write me all details, and frequently; but do not expect long letters from me often.

Give my love to Mrs. Sevier, to Margot and the rest, and you may take a few spoonfuls, if you like,

with only this,

VIVEKANANDA.

PS — Have an eye on the little chap. The boys are already jealous of him. They did spoil another boy that way before.

CCXXV

To Sister Christine

THE MATH, BELUR, DIST. HOWRAH,

14th June 1902.

MY DEAR CHRISTINE,

Your letters had to wait a few days, as I was out of town in a village. Well, many thanks for all the information I got. Mr. Okakura [Kakuzo] has been to the Math, but I was away. He will be in Calcutta a few weeks more and then goes to Bombay. He intends taking a house near the city to learn intimately the customs of Bengalees. I am so glad to learn Margo's [Sister Nivedita's] intention to stop at Mayavati longer. She really requires good rest, and she had none in Europe, I am sure of that. If she were amenable to my advice as of old, I would take away every book and every scrap of paper from her, make her walk some, eat a lot and sleep a lot more. As to talking, I would have the merriest conversation all the while.

I have a beautiful letter from Mrs. Sevier, and [am] so happy to learn that she loves you more and more. But plumpness is the criterion, *mon amie* [my friend], for a' [all] that.

So there was a great flutter in our dovecote owing to my letters, but things must have assumed their old form by this time. The boy, my nephew, is going to be sometime yet in the Ashrama; make him talk English with a good accent — do. No foreign language can be learnt properly unless you talk in it from childhood.

Mr. Bose is still there, I hope; and you must have liked him immensely. He is a *man*, a brick. Tender him my best regards, will you?

Have you any water in the lakes now? Do you get the snows clearer? It has been raining all through this summer here. We had very few burning days, only a number of stuffy ones. Our rains also have nearly set in. In a week the deluge will commence in earnest.

As for me, I am much stronger than before; and when seven miles of jolting in a bullock-cart and railway travel of thirty-four miles did not bring back the dropsy to the feet, I am sure it is not going to return.

But anyway, it is the Math that suits me best just now.

With all love,

VIVEKANANDA.

CCXXVI

To Sister Christine

THE MATH, BELUR, DIST. HOWRAH,

15th June 1902.

DEAR CHRISTINE,

Just now received your note. I am quite easy in my mind so long [as] you live with Mrs. [Charlotte] Sevier at Mayavati. You know, anxiety is one thing I must avoid to recover. I will be very anxious if you are in Calcutta, at Baghbazar. I am slowly recovering. Stay with Mrs. Sevier as long as you can. Don't come down with Margot [Sister Nivedita].

With love,

VIVEKANANDA.

CCXXVII

To Sister Christine

THE MATH, BELUR, DIST. HOWRAH,

21st June 1902.

MY DEAR CHRISTINE,

You have not the least cause to be anxious. I am getting on anyhow and am quite strong. As to diet, I find I have to restrict myself and not follow the prescription of my doctor to eat anything I like. The pills continue, however. Will you ask the boys if they can get "Amalaki" [*Emblic myrobalan*] fruits in the place now? We cannot get them in the plains now. They are rather sour and puckery eaten raw; but make marmalade of whole [ones] — delicious. Then they are the best things for fermentation I ever get.

No anxiety on the score of Marie Louise's arrival in Calcutta. She has not yet made any noise.

Things go on the same. I am trying to go to Monghyr — a place near Calcutta and said to be very salubrious.

We will think of your coming to Baghbazar after Nivedita has fairly started; till then keep quiet and lay on food.

With all love to yourself, the boys and Mother [Mrs. Charlotte Sevier],

VIVEKANANDA.

PS — I am laying on adipose tissues fast — especially about the abdominal regions: "It is fearful to see!"